THE
ENVIRONMENTAL
ECONOMIC
REVOLUTION

THE ENVIRONMENTAL ECONOMIC REVOLUTION

HOW BUSINESS WILL THRIVE

AND THE EARTH SURVIVE

IN YEARS TO COME

MICHAEL SILVERSTEIN

ST. MARTIN'S PRESS NEW YORK

DESIGN BY JUDITH A. STAGNITTO

ISBN 0-312-09797-2

First Edition: September 1993

10 9 8 7 6 5 4 3 2 1

CONTENTS

THE
ENVIRONMENTAL
ECONOMIC
REVOLUTION

ONE

INTRODUCTION

Some people think that preserving the natural environment will emerge as the central organizing principle of the twenty-first century. Others believe that ecological damages are becoming so extensive, "the environment" will turn out to be the central disorganizing principle.

For better or worse, however, attempts to grapple with man-made environmental upheavals spawned in this century will play an extraordinarily important role in shaping events during the next hundred years of human history. This process will not only entail enormous changes in individual orientations but will mandate a vast restructuring of long-established institutions.

This greening effect is already noticeable in the current responses of human institutions to such global problems as atmospheric warming and ozone depletion. Though disagreements persist concerning the immediacy of these macroenvironmental threats, many of the world's leading scientists are already actively addressing them, and huge amounts of intellectual and material resources are being allocated in support of their efforts.

Changes linked to the environment are even more apparent at the national and regional levels. And how could it be otherwise?

The evidence of industrial pollution as a factor undermining societies throughout Eastern Europe is available for all to see. So, too, are the consequences of environmentally destructive agricultural practices in areas as diverse as sub-Sahara Africa and the islands of the Caribbean.

In parts of the world like our own, where the most blatant environmental damages are rarely on view, the effects of pervasive pollution (and attempts to check its spread) now turn up in countless situations. Symptoms of these problems are visible in the size of a homeowner's water and sewer bills, the difficulty many people have breathing when local air inversions compound the effects of local smog, in the spills and discharges that periodically despoil beaches.

Signs of budding solutions to these problems are visible as well: in the new green curricula starting to appear in grade schools, in the increasingly earth-friendly packaging of goods sold in supermarkets, and in the consciousness-raising subject matter of so many new books and nightly television shows.

Virtually everywhere one looks today, in fact, an environmental concern or consequence seems to be hovering somewhere in the background, if not yet actually on center stage. And almost always, these same concerns and consequences are bringing about subtle—and not so subtle—changes in some institution or other.

Established religious doctrines are taking on a greener cast, which makes them less hostile to environmental preservation, at the same time earth-centered "native" faiths are enjoying revivals. Much of the politicking in the United States now involves decisions with an environmental impact, while in some nations of Eastern Europe with profound ecological problems, an ecofascism linking motherland salvation with hostility toward motherland-destroying "outsiders" is stirring.

The arts, legal systems, social customs, fashions: All these institutions are also accommodating to new environmental imperatives in different ways, at different speeds, in different parts of the world.

This phenomenon may be viewed as a good thing, or as yet another irritation contributing to the pool of human misery. Regardless of one's preferences in this realm, however, it is clearly a factor whose importance cannot be ignored.

Environmentalism is no longer just a concern of ecologists, moralists, and nature lovers. Over the last two decades, it has evolved into a mighty force generating change across the entire spectrum of human activities.

Institutions that emerged in earlier times when nature was considered a given, a fixed set of norms within which people could behave more or less according to their own tastes, are being churned into dramatically new configurations everywhere in the world as natural systems are polluted into a state of man-made flux. The intense interactions between people and nature, which for so long badly undermined the health of the latter, are today taking an even greater toll on the lives of the former.

Many writers and commentators have attempted to discuss this complex new reality. In his book, *Earth in the Balance*, for example, Vice-President Al Gore undertakes what he calls "an investigation of the very nature of our civilization and its relationship to the global environment." This is the big-picture approach to the changing role of the environment in human affairs.

A less ambitious but more focused way to tackle this subject is to consider the effects of new environmental imperatives on a single set of institutions in a single national context. Such is the approach employed in the following pages.

This book is about the environmental restructuring of economic institutions in the United States. It describes how environment-linked factors are fundamentally altering the value of assets, the way products are made, the material that goes into their manufacture, the kinds of things people buy, the way in which managers and planners function. It describes, in essence, a set of changes so profound, they can literally be said to constitute a second stage of the Industrial Revolution.

In order to get across these points, our early chapters first examine why both economists and environmentalists in years past have failed to appreciate these changes, while some leading members of this country's business community have been quicker to do so.

We go on to look at the specific ways in which the U.S. economy is being environmentally restructured. Included are greening profiles of a dozen key business sectors (petrochemicals, banking, utilities, insurance, aerospace, agriculture, et cetera), and a look at the huge environmental cleanup industry that has come into being on these shores since 1970.

Changes in the way goods are packaged and sold, as well as manufactured and distributed, along with what "going green" means to this country's immensely generative and creative small business sector, are considered in chapters 4–6. The aim of these marketplace overviews is to demonstrate the extraordinary scope and pervasive influence of environmental factors in the current functioning of the U.S. economy.

In Chapter 7 we consider how these vast economic changes are affecting the local and regional economies in different parts of the United States. To illustrate how culture-specific is the phenomenon of environmental restructuring, we examine in Chapter 8 how it is being played out in such foreign countries as Japan, the lands of the old Soviet Union, Germany, and Mexico.

Everyone must eat to live, but there are striking differences in the cuisines of different nations. Every national economy today is obliged to adjust to new environmental realities, but each reacts at its own pace and in ways strongly influenced by indigenous factors. Just as industrialization initially took hold differently in different parts of the world, the move from pollution-based to environmentally sensitized economies is proceeding along equally diverse lines.

Chapters 9 and 10 suggest policies that government and business can follow to accommodate the challenges of a greening marketplace and the distractions to be avoided along the way. Also included are some observations about the pain of change, a pain that is so much a part of the current economic greening.

Too often, when the topic is economic evolution or newer forms of economic production that replace outmoded ones, something gets overlooked in the argument—those people who cannot or will not change to meet the times. Every revolution has its winners and losers. Each creates a turbulence that some people see as a frightening set of problems and others welcome as an enriching series of opportunities. Certainly, these observations apply to the green economic revolution. One reason for writing this book is the hope that a better understanding of the process at work here will help more people become beneficiaries of this revolutionary transformation rather than its victims.

A final preliminary observation should be made about the tone employed on these pages. This book is *not* written as a utopian tract, nor does it fit into that category of environmentalist literature which seeks to reinvent the economy in order to save Mother Earth. It describes a set of already well-advanced, largely market-based rather than regulation-based changes, which collectively constitute a new economic reality that *today*, not in some distant unsustainable future, make synonymous environmentally and economically sound behavior.

That this new reality has not yet been fully appreciated by environmentalists, economists, government planners, many members of the business community, and the American public in general, is the primary failing this work seeks to correct.

A BRIEF HISTORY

The new environmental economics described in the following pages, the new relationship between environmental health and economic wealth, is a set of views so inherently simple and obvious that it can be reduced to a single equation:

What's good for the environment = What's good for the economy

Like any mathematical equation, this one makes exactly the same sense when the statements on either side of the equal sign are reversed:

What's good for the economy = What's good for the environment

If this relationship is so simple and obvious, one might ask, why has it not been a commonplace belief among government planners, business executives, economists, and environmentalists for many years? And why, even today, do these groups still so often anguish about "making the hard choices" when it comes to protecting the environment and promoting economic development?

The answers to these questions are to be found in history. More specifically, they are to be found in the deep schism that opened in the nineteenth century between defenders of nature and proponents of economic growth, and in the healing of this schism that is only now taking place.

Today's environmental economics, in other words, has yet to free itself fully from the contradictory and confusing environmental economics of times past. An obvious contemporary synergism between environmental and economic well-being is still obscured by long decades of ideological smoke and fluff, and by the dead weight of intellectual traditions that have not kept pace with changing realities.

The primary thrust of the original Industrial Revolution was to change the emphasis in advanced economies from agriculture and commerce to manufacture and technology. This transition is usually said to have begun in England in the mid-eighteenth century; however, it only really took hold there and in the rest of Western Europe (as well as in the United States) in the early part of the nineteenth century. Since then, the Industrial Revolution has spread gradually around the globe.

Two sharply differing romantic reactions to the excesses of this vast economic drama emerged in the mid-1800s: socialism and environmentalism.

Socialism, along with classical capitalist theories of the same period, easily accepted the injuries inflicted on nature in the course of expanding industrial production as a minor price to pay for "progress." Such acceptance was possible because the economic penalties of pollution were not then apparent.

Everyone who lived in London during the latter part of the nineteenth century, of course, personally experienced the horrendous effects of air pollution because of the dirty coal used to heat buildings in the city. The same was true in industrialized areas throughout Europe, where the air literally stank. Nineteenth-century economists, however, ignored such pollution in their writings because it seemed to involve no particular economic drawbacks.

The air always seemed to clear itself after a time, in any

case—if not over a city proper, then just ten or twenty miles outside city limits. Rivers eventually carried away sewage and industrialized filth, to seas and oceans whose size seemed to make them impervious to permanent damages inflicted by human polluting practices. And if the land did seem to be showing signs of exhaustion or excess contamination, people could always move to the New World, where there was still plentiful virgin soil and other resources to exploit.

Such thinking made excellent sense to the eminently sensible people who created classical economic theory. Indeed, in the period when this theory was largely being created, it was a fair reflection of observable reality.

During the nineteenth century, the world had a human population of less than 1 billion, industrialized societies produced relatively simple carbon-based pollution, and industrialization was limited to a few countries in Europe and North America. Economists could thus more or less ignore the environmental implications of economic activity and focus their thinking elsewhere.

What resulted was a kind of "above-the-navel" economics dealing exclusively with "higher" functions such as wealth creation and distribution. It took virtually no notice of the back end of the economic cycle, because a mysterious personage seemed to take care of all *that* sort of thing, in much the same way that the "invisible hand" postulated by economist Adam Smith seemed to set prices properly and reward people appropriately when a marketplace was allowed to operate unfettered.

Karl Marx and other socialist thinkers of his time completely accepted this view of things. Their objections to pollution-based production, in fact, had nothing to do with its consequences for nature—an entity then widely regarded as something humans had a right, and even an obligation, to tame. Socialist objections to early industrialization were based solely on the manner in which newly created wealth was distributed among different classes of society.

This disdain for nature vis-à-vis economic progress was therefore pursued with a vengeance after socialist governments came to power in our own century. In large measure, it explains why ecosystems in the former Soviet Bloc countries of Eastern Europe and other lands strongly influenced by socialist economic theories became environmental basket cases in our own time, even more so than in many capitalistic countries, where individual landowners at least protected large tracts of their own property from industrial "progress."

Environmentalists' hostility to excesses of the early Industrial Revolution was as intense (if not nearly as politically powerful) as that of socialists, but directed in a totally different direction. People with a strong feeling for nature, who saw industrial wealth being created in sprawling manufacturing centers at the expense of the air, the water, and the soil, drew a simple conclusion: Any modern means of creating wealth—socialist or capitalist—was anathema to the natural order.

This reaction, in turn, led to a generalized and often ferocious antimaterialism—at least materialism of the kind found in cities and generated by a new entrepreneurial class. A legacy of this reaction to "satanic mills" and the sooting of once-green valleys was Luddite environmentalism, a hatred for modern industrial society and the material wealth it produced.

Since many of the most vocal mid–nineteenth-century environmentalists were substantial landowners seeking to protect the pastoral purity of their own property, however, this reckoning tended to exclude materialism based on old inherited commercial and agricultural wealth. And since the environmental organizations that sprung up at the end of the nineteenth century also quickly attracted the scions of *nouveau* wealth derived from high-polluting activities such as mining, petroleum exploration, and railroad building (people laundering fortunes brought into being by a family fortune founding ecobeast), the antimaterialism bias of organized environmentalism coexisted quite cozily with the Rockefeller set.

From the first, therefore, organized environmentalism exuded an aura of social caste and economic class, and was steeped in a not-always-subtle hypocrisy. Its most prominent agents tended to preach a brahmin do-goodism that asked the great unwashed to stay poor in order to save nature.

Economically speaking, in fact, environmentalism emerged as the doctrine of the already well off directed against upstarts who had not yet ascended the ladder of material success. It was an expression of the exalted sensibilities of a manor lord directed against the predations of impoverished poachers who wanted something to eat before extolling the beauties of nature.

This antipopulist elitism, though much moderated today, is still alive and well. It largely explains why environmentalism as a political force is strongest in prosperous suburban areas and weakest in impoverished inner cities, and why environmental movements are so important in setting political agendas in rich parts of the world and near the bottom of national priority lists in other places.

Progress ideologues, nature mystics, and gentried dilettantes set the tone of the environmental economic debate in this country and the rest of the industrialized world during much of the nineteenth century. And the terms of this debate were stark. You could be "modern" and enjoy the fruits of materially enriching contemporary technologies, or you could be a romantic defender of a threatened natural heritage.

This hard-edged model began to be revised about the turn of the twentieth century. The unbridled robber baron exploitation of the United States, the attitude that you could do anything you wanted to nature and hang the consequences, began to be modified somewhat in this era.

There were two main threads in this revisionism in the United States. John Muir, founder of the Sierra Club, led a crusade known as "preservationism" whose aim was to ensure that as much of the nation's natural beauty as possible would remain unchanged and unspoiled forever. Gifford Pinchot, Yale School of Forestry founder and a close associate of Teddy Roosevelt, headed a movement called "conservationism," directed toward intelligent land management and wise use of the nation's natural resources so these could generate wealth for Americans in perpetuity.

The collective efforts of these two visionaries and their fellow environmental activists was an arrangement that might be summed up: Give unto Gaia that which is Hers, and unto Mammon-developers that which is theirs.

Gaia got the national parks. The developers got everything else. In places where this "everything else" included tracts of forest or other potentially renewable resources, however, economic development was to be managed so as to conserve its wealth-generating capabilities.

This first-wave twentieth-century environmental economic revisionism affected only a relatively few industries, such as forest products and mining and, to a lesser extent agriculture, stock raising, and fishing. Though initially opposed by leaders within these industries, it was gradually accepted by these same people. They came to recognize its limited geographic and economic scope, its long-term benefits for their business investments, and its personal advantages to their lives as sportsmen and property owners.

Into a nineteenth-century fabric of environmental economics, woven exclusively of clashing antimaterialistic Luddism and unbridled exploitation, was thus added turn-of-the-century threads of conservationism and preservationism.

These additions made it possible for George Bush in 1988 to proclaim himself "the environmental President." In the sense that being environmental meant protecting John Muir's national park system and the natural beauty of coastal Maine, while fostering fellow Yalie Gifford Pinchot's views about progressive land management, President Bush qualified. Indeed, Bush administration environmental policies during the late 1980s had much in common with Teddy Roosevelt's Progressive Party platform of 1912.

In a related vein, so-called wise use groups that today vehemently oppose the efforts of environmentalists to restrict logging in the old forests of the northwestern United States also can claim to be following in the Pinchot tradition. What they are seeking to destroy is, after all, something that will eventually renew itself in *some* form—though as ecologists note, not necessarily a biologically diversified one.

This century's second major revision of environmental thinking with enormous economic implications began to take hold in the 1960s. It involved a process of democratization, both in terms of how it defined "the environment" and in the number and types of people attracted by this changed perspective.

The most important visionary here was a marine biologist named Rachel Carson. Her 1962 best-selling book, *Silent Spring*, was about the widespread destructive effects of insecticides such as DDT. In a larger sense, however, the book described how the entire world environment, not just the nature preserve areas of interest to preservationists and conservationists, was at risk because of pollution spawned by modern manufacturing and agricultural practices.

As Carson's influence spread, people began to see "the environment" in a much more all-encompassing light. One no longer had to be a nature lover or a sportsman to perceive the necessity of protecting ecosystems. To many, quality of life suddenly mattered as much as quantity of production. Our continued physical health, as well as our spiritual well-being, became popularly linked to the endangered health of the larger ecologies in which we dwell.

Ripples (and sometimes tidal waves) from these extraordinary insights continue to the present day and will doubtless do so for many years to come. In Carson's own time, the political and economic repercussions were immediate and profound.

A mass movement sprang up demanding that environment-destroying policies of all kinds be changed. And the manner in which these changes were expected to take place was *very* strongly influenced by the political attitudes toward business and government that happened to prevail at the time.

This was an era of unprecedented prosperity and optimism in the United States. The children of a widely diffused affluence were bored with "success" and "corporate conformity" and the accumulation of "things" generally. The chance to join a movement that not only promised to save the world (literally), but that permitted rejection of the acquisition ethic that dominated the lives of their parents, had enormous appeal for young people of the Sixties' Generation.

Because American corporate profit-oriented culture was so closely associated with newly appreciated threats to natural ecologies, being anticorporate was part of this movement's ideology from the first. The fact that American corporate attitudes toward a larger environment beyond national parks was a simple reflection of overall American attitudes did not in the least modify this article of the new environmentalist faith. A good scapegoat is crucial to any budding movement, and "Corporate America" played the role nicely for this one.

Another tenet of this New Age environmentalism was a belief that government was the primary tool to make things better. This idea was related to the period's Great Society mentality. If there was poverty, government programs would eliminate it. If there was pollution, government regulations would make it go away.

The environmentalism that blossomed in the late 1960s and early 1970s, then, featured elements that combined young people's rejection of their parents' money-making values with an idealistic quest for rustic simplicity in contrast to a perceived cult of corporate greed. It was a kind of neo-Luddism, practiced by middle-class kids with college educations who grew up thinking that everything would always get better and that they were guaranteed a comfortable standard of living any time they opted to "sell out" and trade in their jeans for business suits.

A few nature gurus and a hodge-podge of liberal agenda advocates provided the ideology for this movement. Its negative views about the intrinsic worth of growth as an economic goal was exemplified by the title (if not necessarily the content) of a popular book of the period: *Small Is Beautiful*.

The pivotal year for this Woodstock-era environmental economics was 1970. This was the year the first Earth Day was celebrated, the year the Environmental Protection Agency came into being, the year the first pieces of modern environmental legislation—the National Environmental Policy Act and the original Clean Air Act—were passed by Congress.

Between 1970 and 1980, another half-dozen key federal environmental initiatives became law. The Safe Drinking Water Act (SDWA) was passed in 1974; the Clean Water Act

(CWA) in 1977; the Hazardous Materials Transportation Act (HMTA) in 1975; the Resource Conservation and Recovery Act (RCRA) in 1976; the Toxic Substances Control Act (TSCA) in 1976; and the Comprehensive Environmental Response, Compensation and Liability Act (CERCLA, or the "Superfund" law) in 1980. The Occupational Safety and Health Act of 1970 (OSHA) also had many provisions with an environmental edge.

In this same decade, state and local governments passed hundreds of new environmental laws. Environmental bureaucrats at all levels of government issued thousands of new regulations, and the courts rendered myriad environment-protecting decisions.

Collectively, these laws, regulations, and court decisions began to have a profound impact on the overall operation of the U.S. economy. Companies in scores of high-polluting industries were obliged to start changing traditional modes of operation, often with difficulty and almost always with ill-grace.

Because polluting companies in the late 1970s and early 1980s resented these changes and were very vocal in railing against them, the notion that being pro-environment meant being antibusiness was reinforced. And since the most visible force working to environmentally sensitize business was government regulation, the "greening" of the economy came to be seen as primarily a regulation-driven, rather than a market-driven, phenomenon.

By the mid-1970s, American government had emerged as a mediating, balancing, and, not infrequently, facilitating agent for two officially recognized but largely irreconcilable environmental economic visions put forward by the save-the-environment-at-all-costs and the pollute-we-must establishments. Each vision had its own media and economist retainers. Each had its own affiliated for-profit and nonprofit special interest supporters.

The ideologies of these competing visions were a jumble of historical baggage and pop mythology, along with antagonistic value systems and assessments of who should pay the environmental cleanup piper. These visions included elements of populism and elitism, fabianism and free enterprise, individual and collective responsibility, quality and quantity measurements of progress. They even had religious overtones in conflicting ideas about nature as the dominion of people as opposed to nature as an object of human stewardship.

The only thing these competing visions seemed to share was a belief that economic development and environmental protection were incompatible goals. Like Communists and Fascists, who for decades disagreed about everything except that society was a struggle among classes, establishment environmentalists and their establishment pollute-we-must opponents both went along with the single premise that as a nation, we had to make a fundamental choice between environmental protection and economic well-being.

Both parties clung tenaciously to this view, for years after it had lost ecological validity and economic substance. And so did the elected and unelected officials who acted as their political instruments in Washington.

The Reagan administration came to power in 1980 at a time of great public disenchantment with government and post–oil shock stagflation. Not surprisingly, therefore, its policies embodied views of the pollute-we-must crowd perfectly.

It was fiercely antiregulation, which its backers interpreted to mean it was pro-business. It favored a wise-use populism, as defined by people who deemed unwise any restrictions on their rights to use land or resources.

The Bush administration, which came to power in 1988, started out with a slightly different orientation, reflecting its leader's patrician background and longtime identification with the Republican Party's monied, ecopaternalistic, East Coast Teddy Roosevelt wing. Soon enough, however, Bush initiatives succumbed to the earlier Reagan approach toward environmental economics.

Why this backtracking by Bush? Traditionally, when times get tough, Republicans blame it on regulators and do whatever they can to not upset business interests of any kind. Times started to get very rough by 1990, and the flagrantly misnamed Council on Competitiveness then began to dominate the Bush administration's environmental policies. In the guise of freeing business from the burden of regulations and thereby boosting employment and profits during a recession, this Star Chamber for congressionally approved environmental measures, a carryover from the Reagan years, abetted polluters unwilling or unable to meet new green market challenges.

A patina of intellectual legitimacy for the council's efforts came from abroad. As Soviet power unraveled after 1990 and the extent of environmental damages in that empire came to public attention, the Bush administration claimed this as proof that state power as a mechanism to protect the environment was a road to failure.

The Soviets had no free enterprise and horribly damaged ecosystems, this wobbly ideological argument ran, while we had lots of free enterprise and much healthier ecosystems. Free enterprise, defined as unregulated business, was therefore "proven" the best solution to pollution.

That environmental laws and regulations throughout Communist Eastern Europe had been almost totally ignored (where they existed at all) made no difference to proponents of this argument. Nor did the fact that the regulations in the United States that they were seeking to undermine were largely responsible for preventing the Eastern European–style environmental holocaust they purported to abhor.

No matter. Everyone knew in these years that the choice was between environmental protection and economic growth. Reagan-Bush policies were merely the Republican Party's late-twentieth-century way of pursuing the more desirable of these mutually exclusive goals.

The penultimate absurdity of this approach occurred in June 1992. So politically committed to the Gaia-versus-Mammon paradigm had the administration become by this time that President Bush almost opted not to attend the United Nations' Earth Summit in Rio de Janeiro, Brazil. As it turned out, his attendance at this event became a mammoth embarrassment, as he stood almost alone in refusing to sign treaties virtually

every other country of the world regarded as both ecologically
and economically sound.

If those who believed that we had to pollute to prosper held
fast to these views into the 1990s, their official opposition was
equally ossified when it came to the subject of environmental
economics. Again and again in these years, recognized environmental leaders asked people to live more modestly in order to
advance the higher goal of protecting woodlands and estuaries,
of keeping the world safe for timber wolves and snail darters.

They adhered to this either/or model like a talisman. They
flashed it relentlessly, out of genuine conviction or out of fear
that any alteration would confuse the fixed biases of their dues-
paying memberships.

During the 1990 campaign to pass the very comprehensive "Big Green" amendment in California, for example, environmental proponents repeatedly expressed a willingness to
protect that state's natural environment even if it cost jobs—
a notion that opponents easily translated into favoring owls
over people.

A sillier political strategy at a time when California was
fast slipping into a very nasty recession could hardly be imagined. Yet, given the deeply rooted economic philosophy of
organized environmentalists, checking such self-defeating rhetoric proved almost impossible.

Organized environmentalism's major nod to a new environmental economics in the late 1980s and early 1990s was a
push for greater "corporate social responsibility." This nebulous smorgasbord of good intentions called for big companies
to treat their workers well and provide day care and, yes,
pollute less, after signing on to the "Valdez Principles," a set
of politically correct econotions with the inherent staying
power of a temperance pledge in a weekend drunk tank.

Promoting the doctrine of social responsibility as a basis
for environmentally sound corporate behavior was, in fact, a
last-ditch effort by some elements of organized environmentalism to maintain one of their central illusions, a sense of

ethical superiority, in the face of a new truth that threatened to undermine that superior sense of organizational self: the truth that doing right by the environment had become a great way to make a buck.

The New World was not colonized after 1492 to save souls, but to find gold and expand trade. An American did not fly to the moon as part of a great dream of extraterrestrial travel, but to win points in an out-of-control Cold War. This planet's ecosystems are in the process of being saved not by a surge in international ethical standards, but because the marketplace has found good economic reasons to save them.

Nothing in the long history of organized environmentalism had prepared many of its practitioners to cope with this view. So, in the main, they simply ignored it. Only during the presidential campaign of 1992, when candidates Clinton and Gore finally recognized the political necessity of identifying environmental protection with economic growth, did some prominent elements in the American environmental movement finally begin to entertain the possibility that this political need might also have some genuine economic substance.

Language, as well as history, has long muddied the environmental economic debate. Indeed, one of the chief reasons people can still even speak of choosing between the environment and the economy is that they are ascribing meanings to certain key words and terms that are decades (and even centuries) out of date.

Two obvious examples involve the words growth and consumption. In the nineteenth and early twentieth centuries, economic growth was synonymous with bigger and more numerous manufacturing facilities. If you wanted to increase profits and employment, you expanded, you used more raw materials and energy in your operations.

In such an economic ambiance, growth was naturally environmentally destructive. It could not be otherwise since, by definition, "to grow" was to intrude upon and destroy larger and larger chunks of nature.

A very different kind of growth began to appear in the late twentieth century, however. This growth produces many more goods out of the same amount of energy and raw materials through far greater efficiency. It also produces many goods out of recycled materials employing recycled energy.

It creates many jobs and larger profits in service industries rather than in manufacturing—industries that tend to be relatively benign toward the environment, or whose value is closely linked to environmental well-being.

"Growth," in other words, has taken on an entirely different relationship to the environment in our own time. Nineteenth-century pollution-based growth was environmentally unsound and inherently unsustainable. Late-twentieth-century growth is far more environmentally sensitized and, for that reason (at least in theory), infinitely sustainable.

You *can* have it all with this latter-day model because it recognizes that the chief environmental problem with the American economy for many years has not been *over*consumption, but massive and pervasive underconsumption. We actually consume only a fraction of the energy we release. The rest is dissipated and used by no one. We consume most raw materials only once, instead of reclaiming their residual values through all-inclusive recycling in which trash is converted into cash in the process.

The apparent contradiction between high-consumption economic growth and environmental preservation, which has set the economic and environmental establishments against one another since the middle of the last century, thus turns out to be in many respects just a symptom of institutional language lag. Without the proper words, we lose the ability to objectively appraise contemporary reality.

A modern high-growth, environmentally sensitized economy reverses the classic vocabulary, and hence the classic assumptions, of both nature-exploiting "developers" and environmental Luddites. Growth in this new economy comes by squeezing more goods out of the same amount of resources. Profits rise by freeing producers from the back-end costs of

environmental cleanup. Businesses such as tourism, probably
the world's largest industry by the end of this decade (unless
environmental cleanup surpasses it), expand only when the
natural environment tourists wish to visit is properly tended.

The following chapters contain scores of descriptions
showing how this new environmental economics already operates in this country and around the world. A single illustration
here can be used to suggest what lies ahead as this trend becomes ever fully articulated.

The year is 2002. Detroit and other centers of the American car industry are enjoying a banner year, selling 10 million
vehicles. Unlike cars of decades past, however, the vehicles sold
in 2002 are "greenmobiles," which are manufactured in ways
that generate much less pollution than their predecessors.

These cars also run on clean fuels such as natural gas, are
electric-powered, or have very efficient, low-emission gasoline
propulsion systems. When a greenmobile's first automotive
incarnation ends, it is designed to break down into parts that
go into another generation of cars.

The net effect on this country's natural environment of
putting millions of new greenmobiles on the road would be
extraordinarily positive. Such vehicles would replace, and get
off the road, millions of old, pollution-spewing clunkers that
are today the major cause of tainted air in dozens of cities
around the country.

A banner sale year for such vehicles would likewise be a
boon for the American economy. No one, after all, loses work
making greenmobiles instead of high-polluting clunkers. The
same number of autoworkers make the cars. The same number
of dealers sell them. The same manufacturers make profits. The
same consumers have a private car to drive. And even though
certain petroleum companies lose business as part of a greening
that reduces demand for their gasoline, other hydrocarbon
firms are experiencing increasing demand for natural gas to
run cars that use this product as fuel.

Once greenmobiles become the production norm on these
shores, they expand our car exports to countries like Taiwan
and Mexico. Increasingly during the decade of the 1990s, salea-

bility of cars in places like these will depend on environmental soundness that helps counteract effects of local overpollution.

Overall, there is almost nothing that would benefit both this country's economy *and* its environment more than a hugely successful new model year in 2002, during which Detroit sells millions and millions of greenmobiles. "Growth" and added "consumption" here means reduced pollution. This is the essence of a new environment economic nomenclature.

A revolutionary change has occurred in the marketplace in recent years. It is a change ultimately related to the upheaval in all human institutions noted in the introduction of this book. But it also arises out of the internal mechanisms of the marketplace itself.

The nature and implications of this change were largely overlooked (or at least downplayed) by establishment interests imprisoned in the intellectual amber of their own histories, ideologies, vocabularies. Until 1992 electoral politics began to impose this new perspective on the American mainstream, most people at the top of our national political and economic power structures were ill-prepared to recognize and appreciate the importance of this revolutionary new environmental economics.

It therefore initially blossomed in this country as a bottoms-up rather than a top-down phenomenon. The first people fully to appreciate its existence and the opportunities it represented, to understand that today, not in some fuzzy down-the-road unsustainable future, environmental protection and economic growth are not merely compatible, but absolutely *synonymous*, was a cadre of America's most progressive businesspeople and entrepreneurs. A similar epiphany occurred at approximately the same time among Japan's planning oligarchy (as explained in our chapter "Going Green Around the World").

Both groups are the natural leaders of their respective national economies. Both were happy enough to pollute when polluting was good business and are content to operate differently now that a different set of rules governs the marketplace.

Both today understand that as much money will be made cleaning up the world's natural environment in years to come as was made in all years past polluting this same environment.

Both groups are leading the way within their respective countries in the competition for dominance in a fast-greening world economic order.

THREE

A BUSINESS VIEW
OF THINGS

The health of the world's ecosystems and the wealth of the world's economies now ebb and flow in tandem. The study of this linkage is the new environmental economics. For brevity's sake, this relationship is referred to as *enomics* in the following pages.

Mastering the principles and practices of enomics is already critical in determining the economic success of individuals, companies, and nations. It will become ever more so with the passage of time.

As noted in the last chapter, enomic thinking took hold among certain business leaders in this country before it was appreciated by the environmental community or by the entrenched lobbying and legislative crowd in Washington. The record of economists in this realm also has been laggard.

In recent decades, economists have recognized the need to account for the huge costs brought about by massive pollution, but only in a limited way linked to what is called, in the jargon of their trade, "internalizing externalities" via regulations.

Environmental externalities are costs (such as cleaning

dirty air) created by production that traditionally have been passed on by producers to the general public. Internalizing these costs involves creating a mechanism that forces pollution producers themselves to pay some of these expenses. The mechanism that accomplishes this end is regulation.

It is all too easy, of course, to jump from this sort of thinking to the notion that regulations are a punishment, that they take capital away from projects that might otherwise create jobs and profits, and from these conclusions to fall right back into the old paradigm that we must choose between the environment and the economy. Many economists have so fallen.

Fortunately, the best American executives and entrepreneurs have escaped this particular thought loop, just as they have gone beyond the 1960s' and 1970s' environmentalist version of such thinking. These business leaders have done so because they are far more attuned to current realities than to dogma or ideology.

They function pragmatically in a day-to-day world of markets. Their primary sources of information are not dense studies prepared for specialist scholastics but the daily press, the flow of orders and bills coming in the mail, gossip at trade events, and information contained in the annual reports and 10-Ks of suppliers and competitors. By the early 1980s, America's business elite was seeing something new on its own balance sheets and these other marketplace radar screens: a need to take a fresh look at the environment-economic nexus.

At the start of the 1980s, three basic factors that brought home this changing view became clearer.

- The pervasive effects of a true world marketplace in which there was a far greater need for efficient technologies and management techniques to meet far stronger international competition.

- The emergence of a potent "green" buying preference within key sectors of this international marketplace.

- A dawning realization that government and corporate spending on environmental protection and restoration, over and above the spending generated by individuals' greener buying preferences, had the potential to create a mammoth new set of business opportunities.

These enomic forces grew out of the operations of free markets. They all occurred, however, more or less at the same time that stronger regulations designed to protect the world's ecosystems also were coming into place around the world.

Environmental regulations too, of course, can be considered free-market manifestations, inasmuch as they come into being (at least in this country) because freely elected government officials are giving political expression to their constituents' new marketplace preferences regarding the way goods are made and packaged. Regulations, however, can be viewed in another way as well—not as an expression of changing buyer's preferences, but as a limitation on seller's rights. This latter perception has obscured the true market nature of a greening economic order for many policymakers in government and academia and even in broad sections of the business community.

These people believed, in other words, that only regulations caused an economic greening effect, that this greening was some kind of *artificial* element with respect to a market economy, and that the entire greening process was therefore almost exclusively a discretionary phenomenon. If a government less inclined to push environmental regulations came to power, they believed as late as the mid-1980s, the greening would fade away or at least diminish substantially.

"The environment," in this view of things, was merely a perennial obsession of a group of eccentrics whose influence on market operations was spotty and ephemeral. A sort of economic hives.

Only gradually has this conception given way to a more sophisticated appreciation of what is really happening in the relationship between natural ecologies and the man-made production/distribution/transportation ecologies known as economies. Not only are limits of sustainable growth based on traditional pollution-based techniques being reached in many places around the world, but the internal logic of the market system itself is changing in places like the United States in ways that happen to favor environmentally sensitized operations.

Regulation is part of this process. It helps shape the way the transformation proceeds. It hastens or slows the speed at which different facets of an Enomic Revolution occur. In terms of the overall process, however, regulation is less a master blueprint than a time schedule. Regulations tell you when to expect the train to reach the station—after the track has been laid and the platforms constructed.

Because the most acute and perceptive executives and entrepreneurs in this country and abroad understood the changing nature of environment-linked market imperatives (including regulations) before most other people, by the mid-1980s they were moving to benefit from them. Among this group, "going green" took on a quality not unlike going on a long-overdue diet.

Executives did not undertake this "diet" because they wanted to do it, but because the alternatives were a bloated appearance, a less agile set of responses, or in extreme cases, death. These executives and entrepreneurs might complain about their diet-cum-greening, they might cheat on it from time to time, they not infrequently doubted its efficacy when the pain of pollution withdrawal became acute. In the end, however, in business after business, in industry after industry, greening proved to be not just a necessary but a positive economic experience.

Collectively, in fact, on a national basis, greening was actually the closest thing the United States had to an industrial policy during the 1980s. While self-styled masters of the universe on Wall Street were loading companies up with debt for its own sake, the need to comply with ever stricter environmental regulations and meet other green market imperatives was concurrently obliging these same companies to invest in new plants and equipment that increased productivity as they reduced pollution.

The best and brightest in the American marketplace soon enough realized that what others were lamenting as a "forced," regulation-induced, dietlike change advanced a larger market agenda and their own best interests. They came to identify environmental economics as just plain old good economics; environmental engineering as superior engineering; and environmental management as quality management.

With these realizations came an end to compliance thinking aimed at simply keeping government off their backs and making peripheral public relations points. It was the beginning of a true commitment to getting ahead of the regulatory wave for purely economic purposes.

This appreciation of the enomic potential was at odds with the traditional "environment-or-economy" thinking of the sort that gave rise to Vice-President Dan Quayle's Council on Competitiveness. This council, however, never attracted the best-of-breed in business circles anyway, even at the height of its powers in the early 1990s. Rather, it acted as a magnet for companies unwilling or unable to confront new environmental market imperatives.

Had Quayle's Council on Competitiveness been functioning in the 1890s in the way it functioned in the early 1990s, it would doubtless have been the back-door political agent of blacksmiths and saddle-makers trying to keep government from expanding this country's road network, lest those awful horseless carriages get a foothold in the marketplace and cause mass unemployment in the horse trades. The best American business executives and entrepreneurs in our own times, naturally, would have none of this nonsense.

Once the matter is considered seriously, it is not hard to understand why the internationalization of world markets is so closely linked with the greening of industries in the world's leading economies. The tale begins right after World War II.

When that great conflict ended, there was only one major economic power in the world: the United States. "Buy American" was not just a matter of preference among the world's consumers. It was the only possibility when it came to acquiring many kinds of goods and services.

The productive capacities of Germany and Japan were in

total ruin. Those of England, France, the rest of Western Europe, and all of Eastern Europe were in little better shape. Other countries of the world, meanwhile, were still years away from emerging as serious economic players.

In order to be successful in this post–World War II world, the United States needed only to be a prolific producer. If this production was not especially efficient and consequently highly polluting, so what? There was no one else around who could do it any better.

By the 1970s, and quite dramatically by the 1980s, this set of market conditions had totally changed. Not only had the old manufacturing powers of Western Europe revived, not only was Japan back on its feet and achieving first-tier economic status, but the "young tigers" of Asia and other budding tigers around the world were vying for their own shares of international markets.

With everybody making everything, world surpluses of goods from steel to TVs, from crops like wheat to rice, began to appear. Suddenly economies most closely associated with prolific production (such as the Soviet Union) were impossibly outclassed and being shunted aside by the world's more efficient, more quality-oriented producers.

Though not immediately appreciated, this move toward a market that rewarded the most efficient users of energy and raw materials and penalized less efficient users had enormous ecological implications. Since any kind of waste, toxic or otherwise, is just a symptom of inefficient operations, as the world marketplace became ever more competitive, there was an ever greater economic advantage in the kind of manufacture and transport that pollutes (that is, wastes) less.

Before a largely open, free-market competition among so many nations had materialized, the synergism between economic ascendancy and environmentally sound practices had never been clear. Halfway through the decade of the 1980s, it was becoming very clear indeed.

Why were products of comparable quality from Germany and Japan able to undersell American-made goods so often?

people started asking. It is not because Germany and Japan are today low-wage countries. Japanese worker pay and benefits are about equal to those of their American counterparts, while German workers, on average, get a whopping eight dollars more per hour in pay and benefits than do American workers.

The reason Germany and Japan can pay their people better and still compete in world markets is because they invest heavily in technologies that allow their manufacturers to use raw materials and energy more efficiently. If the United States used its energy resources as efficiently as the Japanese, for example, our national energy bill would be $230 billion a year rather than the $475 billion it was in 1991.

In its broadest dimensions, this new synergism between efficiency and pollution control is easy enough to conceptualize. One need only think of a manufacturing plant. Through this plant runs a pipe carrying noxious gases or liquids under pressure to turn a turbine. There is a hole in the pipe.

When you plug the hole (or wrap a rag around it), two things happen. The pressure increases in the pipe and the turbine turns faster—the plant's efficiency increases. The leakage of gases and liquids stops as well—the plant's air quality improves in consequence.

This is a snapshot of the linkage between increased efficiency and lower pollution. Repeated countless times in newly constructed and modernizing manufacturing facilities around the world, the enomic principle embodied in this snapshot is one of the new factors that increasingly makes a better economy and a better environment synonymous goals.

The next chapter contains numerous examples showing how companies throughout the U.S. economy are today making the critical enomic linkages between ecology-saving pollution reduction and competition-enhancing efficiency. Whether the industry is chemical manufacturing, where a firm like 3M has saved more than $600 million in recent years by learning how *not* to generate waste, or the utility industry, where electricity sellers like Seattle City Light and Central Maine Power now spend more than 4 percent of their annual revenues to promote conservation, good businesspeople have absorbed the lesson that practices which work to preserve the environment also work to improve their own bottom lines.

As one examines this increasingly pervasive phenomenon, it also becomes clear why it is called environmental economics rather than just plain competitive economics. The principle at work here, after all, is actually nothing other than a straightforward replication of the way nature itself operates.

There is no such thing as waste or pollution in a fully evolved natural ecosystem. Everything discarded or emitted by one species ultimately becomes feedstock for other species.

When leaves fall off a tree in a forest, squirrels do not leap out from behind boulders with Hefty bags in their mouths, shovel the leaves into the bags with their bushy little tails, then cart them off to landfills. These leaves are not waste. They are a source of sustenance for the trees themselves and for other species in the forest.

In like manner, what we call waste is merely a symptom of an economic system that has not yet fully evolved, fully matured. And what we call pollution is the symptom of an economic sickness that requires treatment.

Just as a greener economy helps nature, therefore, an economy more reflective of "natural" principles generates national wealth. This explains why environmentally sensitized economic systems are more and more being seen as manifestations of a later, more evolved stage of the Industrial Revolution. It is also why companies and nations that pollute and waste less—voluntarily through the vision of their leaders, or involuntarily through forced compliance with environmental regulations—have the greatest chance to survive in today's mercilessly competitive markets.

> Ecologically or economically,
> that which does not change and evolve,
> dies.

The second free-market factor working to green U.S. and world business involves changing consumer preferences at the check-out counter. Chapter 4 discusses these changes at some length, noting not only the rise of ecoretailers but the gradual greening of such longtime retail giants as Sears, Wal-Mart, and McDonald's. Here we need only summarize how this phenomenon affects the general attitudes of product makers and sellers.

Consider in this regard a "typical" green shopper. This person, according to virtually every market survey, is far more likely to be a suburbanite than an inner-city dweller, an upper-income person rather than a less well-to-do individual, a white-collar rather than a blue-collar worker. Even during a white-collar recession, such as the one that hit the United States in the early 1990s, these more environmentally conscious shoppers had more disposable income than people lower down on the economic ladder.

Makers and sellers of products and services aimed at people with higher disposable incomes drew an obvious conclusion from this fact. Whenever a choice is possible between offering a greener or a less green product, go with the greener one—especially since the markup is frequently better as well.

The rationale for sellers in broader mass markets to be more environmentally responsive is different, but equally compelling. Because margins are so thin in supermarkets, discount stores, and other mass market outlets, successful marketers in these settings go to extraordinary lengths to accommodate *all* elements of their prospective shopper base, when this can be done without offending other elements.

This is why those little "k" or "U" kosher symbols appear on so many food products, even though only a small percentage of Americans observe dietary laws that utilize such symbols. The rule of thumb here is simple: Never lose a sale you do not have to lose.

This same rule applies to green buying preferences among consumers of mass market products such as soap suds. If there is any upside to making a product more environmentally acceptable, and little or no countervailing downside, would-be product sellers in a mass market will do whatever it takes not to offend green shoppers.

Over and above a desire to accommodate customers in a

more comprehensive manner, retailers have seen the light when it comes to stocking greener products for other reasons. The great liability net spread by courts and lawyers in recent decades has from time to time ensnared store operators as well as product makers. Thousands of lawsuits, by way of example, have been filed against retailers who sold harmful asbestos products in years past.

With costs to dispose of commercial trash in some parts of the country becoming exorbitant, retailers are working very hard to see that goods shipped to their warehouses are not over-packaged. Bottom-line pressures to display more goods in the same amount of shelf space also make retailers more receptive to items in less bulky packages.

All these trends embody enomic principles. They aim to transcend a waste ethic that has become too expensive to pursue, while promoting maximum possible consumption of space.

A cynic might point out that greener products and greener ways of selling them are very far from being the norm in the United States in the early 1990s. This is true. But no more true than the statement that computer-based inventory control was very far from being the norm in retail outlets in the early 1970s.

Smart businesspeople get on the leading edge of trends. Not the tail end.

A new efficiency imperative is expediting the greening of the U.S. economy. So, too, are pressures from consumers. The third nonregulatory market force at work here is the enormous new economic opportunities being created by increased spending on environmental cleanup in this country and elsewhere—opportunities for people already in the environmental industry and for an even greater number of "outsiders" now exploring its potential.

There has always been some environmental cleanup activity, of course. Someone was always responsible for picking up the garbage and making sure drinking water was safe. Since 1970, however, the amount of money spent in the United States on ever-broadening definitions of "environmental protection" has quadrupled, and this cleanup has changed from a largely public (that is, government) function, to one by and large conducted by the private sector.

Perhaps as many as 2 million Americans now earn a living in the environmental protection field. Some $130 billion is spent annually preserving or restoring the environment of this country, with spending of as much as $1.5 trillion projected over the course of the decade. Worldwide, two or three times that much will likely be expended.

Sums like these cannot help but shape the way an economy (even one as large as that of the United States) operates. Nor can they fail to attract the attention of businesspeople throughout the U.S. economy. By 1991, more than fifty of one hundred Fortune 500 companies surveyed operated divisions or subsidiaries that performed some kind of environmental cleanup function.

Du Pont, long a black hat in environmentalist mythology, has established a subsidiary that applies the company's hard-won experience redressing its own environmental problems to the needs of others. Raytheon, which is looking at declining opportunities in defense contracting, has likewise become very aggressive in this field through several subsidiaries.

One of the apparent paradoxes of today's American environmental cleanup industry, in fact, is the growing importance within its ranks of so many chemical, energy, transportation, and defense companies long known for their own pollution excesses. Though Chapter 5 focuses on environmental cleanup specialty firms, these polluters-cum-polluter-cleaner-uppers also deserve special note because of the reason they are being drawn to this business today.

And what is this reason? The same one that Willie Sutton averred caused him to rob banks. Because that's where the money is.

Groups such as the Business Council for Sustainable Development, the Conference Board, and the International Chamber of Commerce all represent many old-line polluters now pursuing new enomic policies in order to become more competitive, to better serve their clients and customers, and to generate additional income through some form of waste management or pollution control.

Organizations such as the Institute of Electronic and Electrical Engineers (IEEE) and the Society of Logistics Engineers are likewise working greener standards into design and product specifications. In essence, these "specs" will determine how goods (including military goods) are manufactured in this country in years to come. They will thus help determine "where the money is."

The economic future belongs to companies and countries that green their economies fastest and most completely. This enomic transformation is intrinsically bound up with all the key factors now universally recognized as critical to national and corporate economic success: total quality management, increased exports, infrastructure investment and renewal, efficiency in manufacture and distribution, leading-edge technology development, entrepreneurial vitality, full life-cycle planning.

America's best and brightest businesspeople are rapidly working all of these perceptions into their everyday management practices as well as their long-term planning. The favorable economic *and* ecological consequences of these actions would be hard to exaggerate.

THE GREAT GREEN RESTRUCTURING

Du Pont, Exxon, General Motors, Westinghouse, and Pacific Gas & Electric have something very important in common. They all have enormous environmental exposure. All are companies in sectors of the U.S. economy that are now undergoing a profound environmental restructuring. The best and most direct way to understand the actual, here-and-now importance of "the environment" is to look at how firms like these are coping with today's enomic challenges.

Any comprehensive examination of this vast phenomenon, of course, would require scores of detailed and extensive volumes. Indeed, the environmental transformation of an individual firm in, say, the chemical industry, merits its own book.

What follows is thus on the order of a thumbnail sketch, an overview of the greening of a few key parts of a very great whole. It is designed to give a "feel" for the process at work and to illustrate that a force which began in the early 1970s as something of significance to only a few conspicuous high polluters in the chemical, petroleum, and metals industries is now a factor affecting virtually every element of the U.S. economy—including its institutional pillars of banking and insurance and its professions, like medicine and the law.

Even such a modest survey format makes clear how pervasive this greening has become today. How it has evolved from a peripheral "ethical question" to a core business issue throughout the economy. How in large measure it now determines chances for corporate survival among countless American companies, and on a larger canvas, our ability to compete internationally. And why a fast-growing number of American policymakers and business planners now view their (and our) economic futures through a green lens.

TRANSPORTATION

Designing, building, and marketing the "greenmobile" is the make-or-break challenge facing the automobile industry in the 1990s. Such a vehicle would be manufactured in a relatively clean manner that does not generate current fines or down-the-road remediation costs, would run cleanly so as to accommodate greener consumer preferences and tougher government emissions standards, and would be almost completely recyclable when its driving days are over.

Like other heavy manufacturers, carmakers now confront very high compliance costs in their plant operations. In 1989, for example, Ford Motors projected three-year environmental overhead costs of $500 million at its North American facilities. A year later that same three-year projection had been raised to $650 million.

General Motors' environmental spending could be several times this figure over a similar period. GM also has the dubious distinction of being named a potentially responsible party at scores of Superfund sites in different parts of the country. At Chrysler, meanwhile, just to close old facilities since 1988 has cost the company hundreds of millions of dollars in environmental costs.

Accommodating tougher federal and state environmental

standards for cars once they leave the showroom is bringing about its own revolution in automotive design. From front bumpers to tailpipes, from brake linings to cooling systems, car design and construction are reflecting ever greener imperatives.

The most obvious development here, of course, involves propulsion systems. Though GM recently dropped plans to mass-produce its own electric passenger car by the mid-1990s, the Big Three American automakers have entered into a unique electric car development consortium. The consortium will jointly develop better electric car batteries, and it also commits its participants to establishing recharging infrastructure at service stations around the country.

Today all of the world's seventeen leading carmakers have their own electric vehicle programs. Nissan, Honda, Peugeot-Citroën and Fiat are emerging as strong contenders in this field. Mercedes-Benz, by the early 1990s, was probably the world car market's strongest entrant here.

Current approaches in this electric car sweepstakes include battery-generated power, electric power from hydrogen fuel cells, solar power for smaller vehicles, and perhaps even "electric wheel" cars, in which each wheel is separately powered by an electric motor, doing away with several conventional under-hood systems. Chrysler recently announced plans to develop a battery system that charges electric cars as fast as a gasoline-powered car gets a fill-up. Honeywell, Inc. is involved in a venture to make battery charges last longer.

Initially, commercial and government fleet vehicles will be the mass market for many of these technologies. A measure passed by the U.S. Senate in early 1992 called for 80 percent of federal and state fleet vehicles, and 70 percent of municipal and commercial vehicles, to be electric or "alternative" powered by the year 2000. The figure for vehicles purchased by the U.S. military that year is to be 90 percent.

Natural gas–powered cars and trucks, especially for utility company, delivery company, and government fleet vehicles, are already an on-road propulsion reality, especially in California. Many carmakers are now vying for a piece of this burgeoning natural gas vehicle (NGV) market. More than 30,000

NGVs were on the road by mid-1992, with a cost to run today equivalent to only 80 cents per gallon of gasoline.

One interesting variant when it comes to alternative-powered vehicles is the so-called variable-fuel cars that can run on more than one kind of propellant, thereby taking advantage of whatever fuel happens to be selling most cheaply at any given time. By mid-1992 Avis was already offering such cars at its Sacramento, California, airport office. Avis's rental fleet of Chevrolet Luminas can burn unleaded gasoline, ethanol, or any combination of the two.

Truck engines, not surprisingly, are undergoing their own greening, aimed at further reducing smog levels. According to the Environmental Protection Agency (EPA), these smog levels have dropped 8 percent nationally since 1982. Advances in diesel design from Cummins Engine, Detroit Diesel and Caterpillar are expected to contribute to this effort.

American carmakers are certainly not oblivious to the need to produce vehicles that are nearly or fully recyclable when their first driving incarnations come to an end. The companies have been relatively successful recycling the steel and aluminum parts in cars, but considerably less successful when recycling what the industry calls "fluff" materials made from plastics (though the Automotive Group of the American Plastics Council announced plans to remedy this deficiency not so long ago).

Foreign manufacturers are somewhat farther ahead today in the race to produce cars that immediately find follow-up uses through recycling, rather than rotting in the lunarlike junkyard landscapes that are this country's automotive equivalents of elephant burial grounds. BMW and Nissan, for example, already operate disassembly facilities where old cars can be brought in by their owners, sold, dismembered, and sent on for reassembly.

In looking at the competition to create greenmobiles, of course, the international trade implications cannot be ignored. There is now money—lots and lots of money—to be made selling low-emission vehicles in horribly polluted markets such as Mexico City and Taipei.

Additional opportunities in this international green market involve car parts. General Motors recently announced that it had an order from Russia for $1 billion in company-made pollution control equipment.

Automobiles are not the only element of the U.S. transportation network undergoing a greening. Virtually every freight hauler in the rail industry is now seeking a foothold in the solid waste business.

The reason? Solid waste handling mostly consists of carting and burying trash. Railroads not only have the carriers to haul it, but own large tracts of the kind of unsightly real estate usually considered perfect for landfill trash burial. Some experts believe railroads will carry 15 percent of this nation's "urban ore" (trash) to its final resting place by the end of the 1990s.

The environment is also one of the primary reasons natural gas–powered locomotives are being tested today. And it is why magnetic-levitation rail systems (maglevs), which allow trains to travel on a cushion of air above their track base and thus operate more efficiently because of reduced friction, are attracting so much interest. Though maglevs are very expensive to build, they are relatively cheap and very nonpolluting to operate.

According to the Bureau of Labor Statistics, more jobs were lost in the transportation equipment end of the U.S. economy between 1987 and 1992 (229,000) than in any other industry. Greener rail networks, more environmentally competitive with trucks, are clearly being viewed by industry leaders as one way to reverse this shrinkage.

The aerial end of the transportation sector, not surprisingly, is undergoing a greening of its own. Companies like Boeing and Lockheed have the usual pollution control exposure faced by all heavy manufacturers. It is at the level of airport design and operation, however, where some of the most interesting environment-related changes are taking place or being considered.

One such proposal involves constructing runways at a slight slope, so gravity works to reduce fuel consumption at takeoff and again at landing. It has been estimated that as much as 25 percent of the fuel consumed in landing and taking off could be saved by angling incoming and outgoing runways a mere 2 percent.

Such innovations reveal the _real_ essence of green thinking when it comes to technical changes needed to alter economies in ways that also serve to protect ecosystems. The great techno-shifts here almost always involve small, cheap, and simple changes rather than massive investments in exotic new high technology.

Everything in a greener economy changes. But unless one looks really closely, the changes are usually barely noticeable. So everything in a greener economy can also be said to stay the same. This inherently _conservative_ aspect of enomics has been very important in expediting its rapid acceptance over a broad economic spectrum.

UTILITIES

As noted above, utilities producing electricity, along with those selling natural gas, are both moving to get pieces of the private car propulsion business that has long been the exclusive pre-serve of petroleum companies, their gasoline-producing refin-eries, and their gas station–selling subsidiaries. This is just one way in which the U.S. utility industry is feeling the impact of an economic greening. Many others are on view these days to the careful observer.

Simply to meet the sulfur dioxide provisions of 1990's Clean Air Act will cost East Coast and midwestern coal-fired utilities an estimated $4 billion to $5 billion annually. These sums are in addition to a decades-long series of cost runups experienced by coal-using, acid rain–producing electricity gen-erators in all parts of the country.

When it comes to coal and electric power, however, this same coin has another side. Coal is still used to generate about 55 percent of America's electric power, largely because of an ongoing "clean coal" revolution that has worked to make it far more environmentally acceptable.

Environment-linked changes at coal-fired electric plants include using coal from western states that generally has lower sulfur content, enormous improvements in scrubber technology, and even turning coal into a fuel gas that burns more cleanly than the hard black stuff itself.

A number of utilities, such as Philadelphia Electric (PE), are even tapping the recycling potential of higher-sulfur coal. Using new scrubber technology from companies like Allied Signal, PE now produces and sells commercial-qualities of sulfuric acid used in fertilizers as a by-product of its electric power–producing operations.

While coal remains a strong contender in a fast-greening U.S. power industry, nuclear fuel is fading fast. Today the end of the nuclear era in the power industry is in view.

There is a clear analogy here between what happened with nuclear weapons and what is happening with commercial nuclear power. The United States depended on nuclear weapons in its tactical military arsenals between 1945 and 1990, and depended on commercial nuclear-generated power in its national energy policies during a roughly comparable period, running from the mid-1950s through the mid-1980s.

The need for nuclear bombs and shells as tactical counterweights to huge numbers of Soviet tanks became unnecessary, however, once "smart weapons" proved better able to do the job in the war with Iraq and elsewhere. Smart, nonnuclear, antitank weapons had the added attraction of leaving a battlefield that could be occupied immediately, without waiting centuries for radioactivity levels to subside.

Commercial nuclear power plants are proving equally outmoded from the technological perspective. Even with continuous government subsidies in the form of fuel processing and special insurance against catastrophic accidents, the life-cycle costs of building, operating, and especially decommissioning nuclear plants now make them seem increasingly uneconomical propositions.

This explains why in 1991, for the first time in more

than three decades, nuclear generating capacity in this country actually declined. It also helps explain why enrollments in nuclear engineering programs have fallen from more than 2,000 students in the 1970s to only about 1,000 today. The United States now ranks just thirteenth among nations when it comes to deriving its electricity from nuclear sources. (Such sources supplied less than 22 percent in 1991.)

The nuclear power industry was born in the 1950s with promises to one day generate electricity "too cheap to meter." It hit its peak in 1973 when forty-one new reactors were ordered (thirty-two of these orders were later canceled). Its future was sealed with the accident at Three Mile Island in Pennsylvania in 1979. It is now gradually fading from the utility scene. After total government and private spending of almost $350 billion over nearly four decades, the age of nuclear power in this country is being superseded by the age of environmentally sensitive power.

Just as a new mix of technology options and consumer preferences are obliging the American auto industry to focus much of its current efforts on perfecting the greenmobile, a comparable mix is pushing the U.S. electric industry into the postnuclear era. Unfortunately for the utilities that now operate this country's 109 commercial nuclear reactors, attaining a nonnuclear, environmentally sensitized power-producing future imposes very heavy burdens.

The finances of the country's largest nuclear utility, Commonwealth Edison in Chicago, were certainly not improved by costs related to building and operating its last $4.7 billion nuclear generating facility. Nor, for that matter, was the financial situation of Consumer Power Corporation in upper Michigan when a $4.1 billion twin-reactor power plant it had tried to get on-line for seventeen years had to be converted to natural gas.

The multibillion-dollar Yucca Mountain, Nevada, facility, which the Department of Energy is hoping will be a final solution to the problem of housing high-level nuclear waste from commercial reactors, is running into enormous technical and political opposition of its own. Each year it does not do the job it is designed to do costs commercial reactor operators millions of dollars in additional costs to safely store 25,000 tons of spent fuel rods.

Storage is but one of the difficulties with nuclear power that has led some industry experts to question whether *any* older reactor in this country can be operated profitably today. Shorter-than-projected operating lives and soaring decommissioning costs are driving additional nails into this particular coffin.

Many older nuclear plants, it now turns out, will have operating lives of twenty years or less, not the forty-year life spans originally projected. As the costs of decommissioning the Yankee Howe facility in Massachusetts and the corrosion-plagued Trojan plant near Portland, Oregon, are demonstrating, the money set aside over the years by utilities will be woefully inadequate to the decommissioning task.

The Great Nuclear Fiasco is just one way in which electric utilities have learned the hard way that you can't mess around with Mother Nature. She has a way of getting back at you in the long run—right in the pocketbook.

Another costly example of this hard fiscal lesson involves the billions of dollars electric utilities are now spending to replace and clean up the polychlorinated biphenyls (PCBs) in their transformer systems. An environmental albatross with still greater potential to redden utility profits looms in the form of the electromagnetic fields put out by overhead power transmission lines.

A recent study by the Environmental Protection Agency hints at the possibility of a "link" between these power lines and cancer rates among people residing near them. If such a danger proves to be serious, costs to bury power lines could be astronomical.

In a host of other ways, environmental issues are reshaping the way electric utilities operate. Decentralized sources of power supplied by cogeneration are gaining favor. Nature-friendly sources of power such as geothermal, wind generators, and solar farms (including the first large-scale photovoltaic facility now being built in Davis, California) are increasingly popular. New storage technologies are rapidly gaining acceptance.

Conservation and load management (C&LM in utility parlance) are perhaps the most significant new green approaches to meeting customer demand for electricity currently being employed by progressive utilities. Sacramento Municipal Utility District, Seattle City Light, New England Electric, Wisconsin Electric Power, and Central Maine Power already spend more than 4 percent of their annual revenues on promoting conservation. Public Service Electric & Gas Company, New Jersey's largest utility, recently announced its own plan to spend $100 million to reduce consumption by its residential and commercial customers.

Instead of trying to sell power consumers on using more electricity, such utilities have discovered that it often makes much better *economic* sense to sell them on the idea of using less electricity, so that very costly new generating facilities need not be built. This, of course, is a near-total inversion of past utility practices, one brought about in large measure by new environmental imperatives.

Among the many noteworthy conservation initiatives now being pursued by utilities are efforts to make electric lighting less power-intensive. Lighting accounts for about one-quarter of this country's total power demand. Conservation technology available in this field today allows users of more efficient bulbs to get a 20 to 30 percent return on their efficiency investments.

Getting consumers to buy more efficient refrigerators is another popular effort being promoted by power-sellers peddling conservation instead of consumption. Utilities in Minnesota and Connecticut are paying customers to junk their old, inefficient refrigerators.

In the Sacramento area, a utility will give you up to $275 toward the purchase of a new, less wasteful model. A group of utilities has even offered a prize of almost $30 million to the designer and builder of a refrigerator that cuts electric use in half, using no chlorofluorocarbons (CFCs) in the process, and Frigidaire and Whirlpool have entered the competition.

Load management is the other element of the C&LM package. By smoothing out demand for power on their grids, by using ever more sophisticated computer and monitoring equipment, utilities hope to do away with the need to build costly new nuclear, coal, or hydropower plants, while continuing to meet all the energy demands of their customers.

Perhaps the definitive statement of the new relationship governing consumers' need for dependable power, utilities' desire to operate at a profit, government's efforts to maintain a comfortable American life-style, and the biological imperative to protect this planet's ecosystems was summed up in just sixteen words that headlined a September 1992 *Wall Street Journal* advertisement placed by Edison Electric Institute, an industry trade group.

"Protecting The Earth Doesn't Mean Going Without," read the ad. "It Means Making Better Use Of What We Have."

Of such simple statements, placed by such well-established groups, in such high-profile media, are revolutions made—revolutions of a scope destined to make Marxism look like a change in postal rates.

CHEMICALS

The chemical industry is the first industry that comes to mind when most people think of pollution. Almost every major environmental law enacted in the last twenty years has had a significant impact on companies in this field, for the simple reason that about half the 5.7 *billion* pounds of toxic materials the EPA estimates is released into the U.S. environment each year is released by chemical manufacturers.

A typical chemical company today spends the equivalent of 40 to 50 percent of its net income on environmental compliance, on capital expenditures meant to reduce future compliance costs, or on Superfund spending (or set-aside reserves). This is another way of saying that companies in this industry now pay the equivalent of a 40 to 50 percent environmental tax on their bottom lines.

Getting off this compliance wheel, greening the entire chemical manufacturing cycle, and being able to market products that are far less destructive to natural ecosystems are thus what the chemical industry is getting to be all about. When the chief executive officer of a major chemical firm styles himself the firm's chief environmental officer, as many are wont to do these days, he is not engaged in a public relations exercise but stating a simple new reality confronting his industry: green or perish.

Virtually every chemical major is now working aggressively to green its operations in ways that reduce waste as well as lower legal exposure. Much of this activity is related to the EPA's "33/50" initiative, a voluntary effort to reduce emissions of seventeen especially damaging chemicals 33 percent by the end of 1992 and by 50 percent three years later.

Company-specific programs also abound among chemical makers. 3M's Pollution Prevention Pays Program is probably the best known. Since 1975, 3M estimates that cutting waste has saved it more than $600 million in operating costs.

Another chemical maker taking high-profile approaches when it comes to its own greening, instead of passively complying with regulations, is Dow Chemical. Its capital budget for pollution control was approximately $231 million in 1991, $250 million during 1992, and projections of $275 in each of the following two years. Such allocations are aimed at cutting all of Dow's toxic emissions in half by 1995—not just meeting EPA goals set for seventeen contaminants.

In the U.S. chemical industry overall, 11.2 percent of capital expenditures now go into pollution control. Internationally, this is second only to German chemical makers, who funnel 17.5 percent of their own capital spending into this area.

A firm like Du Pont illustrates almost all of the greening trends currently affecting the American chemical industry—for better or worse. Du Pont's total environmental spending rose from about $400 million in 1985 and 1986, to some $900 million in 1990. About $500 million of this latter sum took the form of capital spending aimed at reducing future environmental outlays. By 1993, the company aims to reduce its toxic air emissions by 60 percent from 1987 levels.

A longtime leader in producing the CFCs used in the cooling systems of 130 million cars and in some 80,000 building cooling units, Du Pont is now spending $350 million on facilities to produce CFC substitutes. This market could eventually generate a $6 billion bonanza for companies that successfully produce environmentally sound replacements.

Du Pont's Environmental Remediation Services division may soon be doing $1 billion of business annually, selling to other firms the hard-won environmental cleanup expertise Du Pont itself learned. The company is part of the Plastic Recycling Alliance, which hopes to recycle 25 percent of all rigid plastic containers by 1995. Du Pont is also producing totally recyclable plastic resin fenders that will go on 350,000 Chrysler Concordes in 1993.

Such initiatives and approaches by a chemical maker are certainly not unique to Du Pont. New environmental priorities involving changed ingredients, operating processes, better controls and maintenance, and resource recovery (recycling) are goals the entire chemical industry is pursuing.

Edgar S. Woolard, Jr., chairman and CEO of Du Pont, summed this up neatly not so long ago. "Unless we meet the environmental challenges," he said, "we won't be in business in ten years."

The new environmental economics is as simple as that.

P E T R O L E U M

In the late 1980s, an official of the American Petroleum Institute suggested that U.S. oil companies would soon be spending more on environmental cleanup than on finding or selling petroleum. Such, in fact, was the case by 1990 for Mobil, which spent $950 million on environmental compliance (up from

$780 million the year before) and set aside another $166 million in its Superfund reserve—a collective sum that exceeded Mobil's 1990 exploration or marketing budgets.

In another well-publicized instance of soaring environmental outlays by petroleum companies, Exxon's environmental spending in 1991 rose to about $1.9 billion. This occurred even though the company's Valdez Harbor–related expenses that year were down sharply from those of 1990.

The variety and extent of actual and potential petroleum company environmental liabilities are staggering. They include obligations tied to the operation of refineries, where literally thousands of leaks and spills occur annually. Just to comply with 1990 Clean Air Act standards intended to make gasoline-related emissions less toxic in American cities where pollution is the worst will cost a single refiner, Chevron, more than $2 billion over the next five years. why no new refinery in 20yrs

Environmental problems also touch upon the operation and construction of oil company seagoing tankers, a very high-profile issue in the wake of the Valdez tragedy and major oil spills off the coast of Spain in December 1992 and off the Shetland Islands a month later. These problems include oil company responsibility for damages caused by the estimated half-million leaking underground storage tanks in this country, a goodly share of which are owned by players in this industry. A tank under a local closed-down gas station can easily cost $100,000 to render environmentally sound.

Though the exact extent of liabilities for old, abandoned oil and gas wells is still not fully known, they, too, are a major cost overhang for the petroleum industry. There are some 1.2 million such wells, according to the EPA, an estimated 40,000 to 50,000 of which present serious pollution problems.

Environmental concerns keep oil drillers from opening new fields in Alaska and off both coasts of the lower-48. Concerns about much tougher pollution laws enacted in California and other states, plus worries that many cars of the future will be powered by fuels other than gasoline, are leading many petroleum majors to environmentally reformulate their gasoline products to protect their future market shares.

At a conference held by Yale University in early 1992, an official of the American Petroleum Institute was asked if the environment was discussed at that trade group's recent annual get-together. He thought for a moment and replied: "I don't think anyone there discussed anything else."

America's domestic oil industry, of course, is not facing imminent extinction because of new environmental imperatives. What is disappearing rapidly are industry operators and operations that do not fit comfortably into a greening marketplace.   *oh yea!*

REAL ESTATE

Since about 1620, real estate has been the primary basis of individual and institutional wealth in this country. The various activities that collectively make up the real estate industry have therefore always been the single most important sector of the American economy. Today constructing, developing, buying, selling, maintaining, and rehabilitating properties provides employment directly or indirectly for about one in eight Americans.

"The environment" has turned the entire real estate sector in new directions in recent years. It has changed the materials mix used in buildings, the designs of these structures, the way they are operated, the rules governing their sale. It has redefined terms such as development.

It has turned certain long-held assumptions about what increases real estate values on their ear—such as the idea that more shopping malls and greater population density in suburban areas always work to boost home prices. Today such added development frequently just increases monthly overhead for property owners in a given area, as water, sewer, and other infrastructure maintenance costs boost property taxes, thereby working to lower property values.

Nondevelopment in many areas, conversely, often helps increase these values. Development restrictions in states from

Florida, to Vermont, to California, rules designed to protect the environment, may cramp opportunities for new development, but they work wonders in protecting values of existing properties. The news that a conservancy group has bought adjacent property is the best news a value-conscious landowner can get now in many parts of the country.

It is literally impossible to catalog all the local ordinances and zoning board decisions that have been altered in recent years to protect the natural environment. It is almost as difficult to get a handle on the total number of properties in this country with serious environmental damages, or the cost to remediate these damages. Even a quickie list of these latter real estate problems, however, is awe-inspiring, if not downright terrifying.

Along with the 1,200 or so sites on the EPA's Priority Cleanup List, more than 33,000 additional sites are in that agency's files for eventual cleanup. Depending on whose estimates one chooses to believe, total costs for getting all such properties back into environmental compliance could total $150 billion (the EPA), or $500 billion (the Congressional Office of Technology Assessment), or $1 trillion (some private economists).

State agencies have identified hundreds of thousands of additional "toxic hot spots." And this figure does not include the estimated half-million leaking underground tanks that are largely on petrochemical company lands.

Then there are the building-specific, rather than the land-specific, pockets of real estate pollution. More than 730,000 public and privately owned nonresidential structures are tainted with asbestos, about 20 percent of the country's total.

Lead paint is found in about three-quarters of the homes built before 1980 and today contaminates anywhere from 24 to 60 million American homes. More than 30 million Americans live in cities where pollutants in the tap water exceed government recommended levels of safety. One in five public schools has radon levels that exceed EPA standards. So-called sick building syndrome, a condition involving carpeting, insulation, heat duct dust, and other materials found mostly in new commercial structures, is yet another threat to property values. So are old, deteriorating leaking oil burners in the basements of private homes.

There are all sorts of official, semiofficial, and quasi-official estimates about how much our national asbestos, lead paint, and sick building cleanups will cost. But no one really has a clue about the eventual total outlays that will be required here. Depending on what special interest an estimator happens to be serving at the time he or she makes the estimate, numbers thrown out nowadays run to the tens of billions, the hundreds of billions, or the trillions of dollars.

Industrial properties with old hazardous waste on-site, out back, or even nearby have even more environmental exposure today than residential or commercial properties. Consequently, in New Jersey, an industrial property needs an environmental bill of health before title can even be transferred.

Converting closed-down military bases to private use also is now closely linked to their environmental condition. Plans to convert Pease Air Force Base in New Hampshire were frustrated by disagreements over who would be stuck with the costs of its environmental refurbishment. The Resolution Trust Corporation's own efforts to wrap up the savings and loan bailout have likewise been complicated by environmental problems with some properties the RTC has taken over.

In a purely economic sense, the "health of the land" is a synonym for the selling price of a property. Today this price is being radically affected by environmental conditions. In consequence, builders, developers, property owners, and maintenance firms are all rushing to get on the right side of the green line.

They are doing this by using less environmentally destructive building materials (some made from previously used paper, glass, and even rubber) and disposing of construction wastes in a safer manner. They are designing more environmentally sound structures and entire developments that intrude less on their natural surroundings.

Property owners are learning to avoid the equity risks inherent in allowing land and buildings to be ecologically contaminated. Maintenance specialists are learning the money-saving joys of recycling and are increasingly opting for relatively ecofriendly natural gas heating systems.

The beauty of real estate, as everybody in this business knows, is that they don't make it any more. The real estate industry will thus always be central to the American economy. It will simply be a greener real estate industry, one in which the old secret of success encapsulated in the phrase "location, location, location" is increasingly modified by attention to "pollution, pollution, pollution."

BANKING AND INSURANCE

In part because of their close association with real estate markets, and in part because of other factors, two other longtime pillars of the U.S. economy are going through their own greening process today: banking and insurance.

The vagaries of current and pending legislation, regulation and litigation make it impossible even to guess at the ultimate extent of deep-pocket liabilities banks will be saddled with for environmental cleanup of properties on which they have made mortgage loans. Regardless of developments in this sphere, however, there is no way for banks to escape the equity implications of environmentally blighted real estate.

A building valued at $1 million could be worth half that much overnight if it were found to be heavily tainted with asbestos. A bank with an $800,000 mortgage on such a building might not be forced to pay the asbestos cleanup costs, but it would have to recognize a $300,000 book-value loss.

Some measure of the new importance matters environmental hold for bankers these days could be seen in the program of the 1992 American Bankers Association's (ABA) Security and Risk Management Conference, held in San Diego, California. "Protecting the bank from environmental liability" was the first topic cited in the conference announcement. The ABA has come to regard the risks here as so potentially serious, it even hired consultants to evaluate the burgeoning number of computer software information products designed to protect banks from environmental liabilities.

At virtually every level of the industry, from local neighborhood thrifts to international consortiums, lending policies of banks are reflecting new environmental imperatives. In the realm of international finance, thirty major commercial banks in as many countries signed a United Nations–sponsored "statement on the environment and sustainable development" in May 1992. The statement was billed as the first time such institutions had committed themselves to joint principles aimed at protecting nature.

Another group of international banks, whose charters call for promoting economic growth in underdeveloped parts of the world, have been practicing their own variant of going green in recent years. These multidevelopment banks (MDBs) include the World Bank, the Inter-American Development Bank, the African Development Bank, the Asian Development Bank, and the European Bank for Reconstruction and Development.

The reason such institutions have seen the green light was summed up neatly in a *Philadelphia Inquirer* headline that appeared recently: "World Bank is trying to undo the damage it helped cause."

The damage referred to involves all kinds of jumbo, ecologically intrusive projects the World Bank has funded for decades, right through to the present day. A huge dam project in India on the Narmada River is the current bête noir of environmental critics of the Bank, which dispenses $20 billion in loan largesse to developing countries each year.

Lending institutions more closely associated with the United States government are going green in their own special fashion. The Environmental Aid and Trade Act, first proposed in Congress during 1992, directs government-funded lenders such as the Agency for International Development and the Import-Export Bank to give special emphasis to promoting American environmental goods and services. The primary aim of this legislation is to narrow the nation's perennial trade deficit by boosting exports of environmental services and pollution control equipment.

For better or worse, to the benefit of some and the detriment of others, private U.S. banks are greening their own lending policies. A study done by the ABA in 1990 found that more than three of four banks surveyed were changing their lending procedures to avoid (or at least lessen) environmental exposure.

Loans to companies in certain businesses deemed to be very environmentally sensitive are getting much harder to obtain. This is especially true when it comes to smaller concerns. Some officers at agricultural banks are likewise less inclined to loan money to farmers who use excessive pesticides on their land, and, conversely, more inclined to lend to farmers who do not. Preloan audits before mortgages are granted on residential as well as commercial and industrial properties are becoming a commonplace.

Insurers face their own kinds of serious environmental exposure. Indeed, potential long-term costs to clean up all this country's Superfund sites are estimated to exceed the insurance industry's total reserves.

Anyone who doubts the current importance of the environment to American insurers need only apply for anything approximating comprehensive coverage for a business that has significant environmental risk. It is not available. From anyone. Anywhere.

There are few certainties about how much insurance companies will actually pay when all the legal battles pitting polluters against their past and present insurers are finally decided. In 1986 insurers stopped honoring environmental claims against general business coverage policies they had issued and stopped including any environmental protection in these policies. Since then coverage has been very hard to find, expensive, limited to certain risks, and capped at very modest pay-out levels.

Left open to litigation were the general coverage policies issued during the 1970s and early 1980s, however. The main disputes there involve these policies' "pollution exclusion" clause, and the question of whether pollution damages were incremental or related to a single disastrous happening.

Results of this litigation have been so inconclusive to date that the lawyering could well carry over to another decade. Or perhaps, in the worst *Bleak House* tradition, for several decades.

An insurer in one case was obliged to pay $125 million in toxic waste cleanup on a Texas refinery claim. Another was required to pay $582 million on an asbestos claim. In still other courtrooms, however, an oil company giant lost a court case that would have forced its insurer to come up with $2.4 billion in damages, and a natural gas transmission company lost a court fight to get its insurer to pay $700 million in PCB cleanup costs.

You hire your lawyer. You take your chances.

In one sense, the vaguely grotesque legal game of musical chairs—in which the federal government tries to get state and local governments to pay for environmental cleanups, all governments try to get business polluters to pay the costs, the business polluters try to foist it off on their insurers, while the insurers try to make it a federally funded effort—can be viewed as one of the nation's great public policy spectator sports. In the context of this chapter, however, the game simply demonstrates the visceral importance of the environment to the health of the American insurance industry.

To a not inconsiderable extent, the environment bears a similar relationship to the health of the worldwide insurance industry. Companies such as Lloyd's of London are major players in the reinsurance business, which American insurers depend on to help manage their own risk exposure. And 305-year-old Lloyd's, at the time of this writing, was facing its toughest financial squeeze ever, in large part due to asbestos and pollution cleanup claims in the United States.

HEALTH CARE

Health care accounts for about 14 percent of this country's entire gross national product. And all the major components of our vast national health network are today rushing to cope with growing environmental commitments and obligations.

Health care facilities—hospitals, old age homes, and the like—pay about 4 percent of America's $26 billion-plus annual solid waste handling bill. In addition, these institutions must now pay billions of dollars annually to dispose of hospital-specific "red bag" wastes, which include used syringes, bandages, and isotopes.

The amount of money spent each year to treat environment-related ills and conditions is incalculable. The American Lung Association has pegged the figure for breathing ailments alone at upwards of $40 billion. A report from the Federal Centers for Disease Control and Prevention found that childhood asthma afflicted 4.3 percent of children under eighteen in 1988, up from 3.2 percent seven years earlier. Overall, asthma kills an estimated 5,000 Americans annually.

How much more money is now spent treating ills that come from environmentally contaminated water, exposure to toxic materials in the soil, and other environmental sources can never be gauged accurately. Nor can the extra sums Americans must pay for their medicines because pharmaceutical houses, like all chemical companies, have huge environmental overhead that ultimately gets worked into the prices they charge for their wares.

Along with being a soaring cost factor for drug companies, however, a new environmental sensitivity has had a positive effect. It has led to far more intensive pharmaceutical researches into natural sources for future commercial drugs. Extract from the yew tree as a treatment for cancer is perhaps the best-known recent example of this trend. But many leaders in the field, including Eli Lilly & Company, have become very active in combing the world's rain forests for new drugs that may one day cure human ills.

Consider this example of soaring present-day medical spending. One in six American children under the age of six— some 4 million kids in all, most of them residents of blighted urban neighborhoods—suffer lead poisoning. The cost of treatment for lead poisoning alone for this single age group could soon exceed $2 billion annually.

PULP AND PAPER

In the 1992 presidential campaign, there was a lot of talk about the 32,000 logging jobs that might be lost if companies were not permitted to log the last 10 percent of old-growth forest surviving in the American Northwest. This was a poignant issue for many environmental groups, which are deeply concerned with preserving the biodiversity of this region, as well as for loggers who are concerned about their livelihoods.

But in truth, this dispute is only a footnote to the extraordinary environmental transformation being wrought throughout the entire pulp and paper, forest products sector of the U.S. economy. From planting, to harvesting, to processing, to selling, this industry is undergoing its own greening, as all-encompassing, in its way, as the ones occurring in the transportation, electric utility, and petrochemical industries.

New strains of forest products are being created genetically. New nursery techniques, such as inoculating seedling with mycorrhizal fungi to produce trees better able to survive in environmentally damaged mining sites, are coming into wide-scale use.

New ways of bleaching pulp at mills have reduced dioxin run-offs into waterways by 80 percent in recent years—at least, according to industry estimates (though some environmentalist critics still cite less sanguine numbers). New compositing technologies that substantially increase the strength of wood used in furniture and home-building are being developed to take the place of stronger woods once harvested in old-growth forests that the industry has largely destroyed.

The current revolution in forest management, the greatest series of new approaches since the early part of this century, also has affected ways in which the Forest Service deals with fires in national forests and the proposed changeover from strip-cutting some varieties of trees every century instead of every fifty years.

Perhaps the most publicized element of the pulp and paper sector's greening is built around recycling. The idea of de-inking and reusing newsprint is certainly not new. A printer named Mathias Koops was advocating it in 1800. But it is an idea whose time has certainly come today, for purely market reasons as well as regulatory ones.

Almost 37 percent of all the paper consumed in this country was recycled in 1991, up from less than 30 percent the year before. So much newspaper and other waste paper is now collected that tons and tons have to be exported. Waste paper and cardboard has been the largest export from the Port of New York for several years.

The American Paper Institute now estimates that as much as 42 percent of the paper consumed in the United States will be recycled by 1995—more than 32 million tons in all. The prime bottleneck now is not technology or quality (recycled stock is fast approaching quality levels of virgin material), but the need to build industry infrastructure to handle higher ratios of recycled to virgin feedstock.

MINING AND METALS

Asbestos is the quintessential example of a longtime, very widely used mineral whose economic prospects were virtually destroyed by new environmental imperatives. The Mansville Corporation, once this nation's leading asbestos product seller, emerged from bankruptcy in 1988 only after it agreed to become 80 percent owned by a trust established to pay off asbestos-injury claimants.

The economic fates of hundreds of mining and metal-working enterprises are being affected by environmental considerations today—though few, happily, as dramatically as Mansville. These effects are both positive and negative.

With respect to aluminum-making, for example, the downside when it comes to the environment involves soaring costs of mine cleanup. Reynolds Metals Company was obliged to make capital expenditures related to environmental control of $36 million in the period 1987 through 1989. For the period 1991 through 1994, however, its planned expenditures here will rise to $94 million.

The other side of this coin is that aluminum recycling has long been a highly successful commercial endeavor. By 1989 Reynolds was recycling 450 million pounds of aluminum scrap and paying $180 million to the public to get it. Industrywide, recycling of aluminum cans reached 55 percent by the early 1990s. Aluminum of all kinds is recycled at a 70 percent rate today.

Comparable environment-linked overhead liabilities, along with analogous economic benefits derived from recycling, are to be found in the steel industry. During the late 1980s, a steel-maker like Inland had to spend a whopping $245 million to run its pollution control equipment.

Modernization of steel mills in this country since 1970, meanwhile, even more than a need to comply with stricter state and federal environmental regulations, has worked to reduce air and water pollution in steel mills by 90 percent. The zinc dust produced by electric arc furnaces also has become a valuable, recyclable commodity. On the back end of the steel consumption cycle, more than 100 billion pounds of scrap steel were recovered and reused in 1991.

It is coal, however—the mineral whose mining and use was supposedly doomed by ever-stricter clean air regulations—that best demonstrates the surprising ability of materials deemed environmentally unsound to keep a marketplace niche, provided always that producers learn how to go with the flow by going green.

Today, as noted above, coal is used to generate 55 percent of this country's electricity, up from 46 percent in 1970 when the first Clean Air Act was passed. How was it able to realize this increase when it has for so long been emblematic of pollution?

The $20 billion-a-year industry has invested heavily in "clean coal" technologies, funding largely subsidized by the federal government at the behest of well-connected coal state Congressmen. These technologies include new planting techniques allowing land that has been heavily mined to regain its natural health more rapidly. They also include coal gasification and refining of low-sulfur coal into more commercially valuable hydrocarbons.

And of course they include scrubber technologies. As long as the cost to utilities for coal and the scrubbers that now make its use environmentally acceptable is less than the cost of natural gas or oil, coal mining and coal burning to produce power remains a viable economic and environmental option.

It would be silly to underestimate the potential long-term threat to coal mining represented by environmental worries that include the greenhouse effect and acid rain. Around the world, in fact, from Poland, where a recent proposal to cut coal production because of reduced demand could cost 55 percent of that country's miners their livelihoods, to England, where a government attempt to make even deeper cuts in the native coal industry almost brought down a Conservative government, the greening of the world economy is causing tremors among coal producers.

Again, however, viewed simply from our perspective, the ultimate fate of the coal industry here and abroad is of less interest than the fact that this fate is now so closely tied to new enomic realities.

FOOD PRODUCTION

Many of the environment-linked trends observed in the restructuring of the pulp and paper industry are, of course, also reshaping operations on the 2 million farms that comprise the agricultural sector of the U.S. economy. Because the food produced by the latter is ingested, additional environmental concerns arise here as well.

The effects of chemical pesticides and herbicides on the health of the land, and on the people who farm it, is causing a minirevolution in this sphere. More than one-tenth of the roughly three hundred pesticides currently used on crops in this country may soon be banned by the EPA because of cancer or other health risks. The threat to groundwater supplies from overusing these chemicals is causing both farmers and government officials in several midwestern states to reexamine traditional ways of raising crops.

Farther east, New York City not so long ago "bought off" with a few million dollars' worth of technical assistance upstate New York farmers whose pesticide use endangered that city's drinking water. In California, where allocation of scarce water supplies is arguably *the* most important political issue, rice farmers are learning to flood their fields to clear crop stubble instead of burning this waste, aiming in the process to meet tougher clean air standards while creating additional wetlands.

Though still small in terms of overall crop production, "natural" methods of all kinds are being adopted by farmers around the country. These range from using only organic fertilizers to completely integrated pest management systems that do not employ any man-made chemicals.

Along with cereal grains, other key elements of the American diet are coming (or not coming) to market differently these days because of environmental dictates. Many years of overfishing, for example, have led to a plan in Massachusetts that will dramatically limit catches of cod and haddock. Similar overfishing for deep-sea species such as shark may soon limit the catch there too. All such limits, naturally, radically affect the livelihoods of fishermen.

DEFENSE CONTRACTORS

It turns out that defending the Free World during the Cold War had some very nasty environmental side effects. Thousands of U.S. military facilities in this country and around the world are contaminated with "pink water," a by-product of used munitions as well as chemicals and radioactive materials. In addition, this country's military liberated into the atmosphere a hefty percentage of the nation's total output of ozone-eating chlorofluorocarbons.

The Pentagon's longtime dependence on nuclear deterrence had the unfortunate side effect of littering the American landscape with some of the world's worst nuclear hot spots—and burdening a number of old-line defense contractors with very substantial environmental exposure in the process. Perhaps the best-known offender was Rockwell International, which in 1992 agreed to pay a $18.5 million fine for its work running the nuclear weapons plant at Rocky Flats near Denver.

A fair number of other defense industry heavies may also get hit for some environmental cleanup costs related to old military work for the government. They include rocket engine builder Aerojet General Corp, General Dynamics, Martin Marietta, General Electric, United Technologies, and Lockheed.

On the positive side of the ledger, the superb engineering and design skills developed by U.S. defense contractors during the Cold War have the potential to be transferred to certain environmental cleanup situations. Raytheon, for example, through its United Engineers and Constructors subsidiary, is today a strong competitor for industrial air cleaning projects. The company's Badger affiliate is also a leader in building anaerobic wastewater treatment systems.

Perhaps the most interesting single transformation going on within traditional defense and related aerospace circles today involves efforts by firms to reposition themselves as environmental service providers for their old government employers. Companies that for decades contributed to generating nuclear military waste are now getting substantial contracts to clean up this same material.

On the aerospace front, firms that in years past built intercontinental ballistic missiles (ICBMs) and vied for "Star Wars" contracts are now looking for future profits to earth-monitoring satellites, which help this country and others keep track of spreading deserts and vanishing forests. Other firms are designing "smart highways" that could make auto travel more efficient. In the Pentagon itself, officers who once spoke of the military's mission to protect American interests now speak of protecting its assets (that is, this nation's possessions from pollution damages).

The life-cycle expertise that has been part of Pentagon planning and procurement since the McNamara days of the 1960s is likewise starting to work at eliminating future environmental exposure from today's military projects. In the ultra high-tech realms of America's national laboratories, meanwhile, where once nuclear devices and "smart pebble" antiballistic missile systems were all the rage, spinning out exotic antidotes to environmental poisoning and boosting the economy in the process is the current budgetary strategy of choice.

Everything changes. Everything stays the same.

Pick a sector, any sector of the $6 trillion U.S. economy, and its new enomic orientation quickly becomes apparent. In the next chapter we focus on how this phenomenon is being played out in the economy's consumer product-making, packaging, and retailing realms.

SELLING THE GAIAN WAY

Perhaps no element of a greening U.S. economy is more misunderstood than the manner in which product selling in this country is being reshaped by a need to accommodate "the environment." Green marketing is still treated as a fad by many commentators, a sort of super–lava lamp buying quirk that generates sales for a while in a few markets, then fades away when a new mania catches the consuming public's fancy.

This notion, it must be admitted, does have a certain historical substance. Right after the first Earth Day in 1970, there was a huge burst of interest in selling all kinds of "earth-friendly" products. Such activity waxed during the 1970s, then waned with the arrival of the first administration of Ronald Reagan.

When a resurgent environmentalism gave rise to another round of green marketing in the late 1980s, the initial reaction of marketing pros was: Here we go again. How long will it last *this* time?

The experience of some environmental product purveyors in the early part of the 1990s seemed to justify this cynicism. A feverish burst of green marketing accompanied the twentieth-anniversary celebrations of the first Earth Day in 1990. By May 1992, however, the *Wall Street Journal* was running stories headlined " 'Green' Product Sales Seem To Be Wilting." The following month, a highly respected trade publication, *Advertising Age*, ran an entire section entitled "Is Green Marketing Dead?"

Green marketing, it turns out, is *not* dead in its present incarnation. Nor is it likely to expire any time in the foreseeable future, according to most experts queried by *Ad Age*. At the same time, these pros also cited noteworthy changes in the nature of the beast.

The original meanings of terms such as green and earth-friendly as applied to products during the 1970s are today, by and large, passé, as are many green marketing techniques favored in that period. Producers can no longer merely put an earth logo on a product label, color it leafy, add some cloying notes about disappearing rain forests or dying seals, and expect good-hearted environmentalists automatically to buy. As the public's sophistication about the complexity of melding human material wants with ecological necessities has grown, so, too, has the complexity of green marketing.

The 1990s buying public has shown itself to be resistant to higher prices based on little more than a manufacturer's assertion that a product is "environmentally sound." Government agencies these days also are showing a positively hostile attitude to egregiously exaggerated green labeling claims.

Once these new difficulties are recognized and accepted, however, the reality of green product manufacturing, packaging, and retailing (the three elements that collectively comprise the enomic marketing phenomenon) become quite clear. The only fad thinking here is the notion that such realities will disappear or lessen in importance over the course of time.

In the discussion of enomic marketing that follows, we focus more on an overall process at work than on specific ways in which this process is currently expressed. It is less important from the enomic perspective, for example, whether more products and their packaging are ultimately designed to be biodegradable or recyclable or simply less voluminous (a major point of debate within the environmental community) than that these same products and their packaging are increasingly designed to be one of these three because of "the environment."

This never used to be the case. It therefore represents a new enomic marketing reality.

We are also less concerned about whether a majority of buying decisions are now influenced by environmental considerations than that a growing number of these decisions are so influenced. A marketplace is not an election. The only number of consequence in a two-person political race is 50.1—the percentage that provides a margin of victory. Within a consumer market, however, sellers cannot afford to lose 20 percent, or 10 percent, or even 2 percent of their potential customer base because of perceived environmental insensitivity.

Looking beyond specifics and focusing on more general trends thus helps eliminate some of the confusion encountered in trying to analyze results from the many environmental market surveys that have appeared in recent years. A host of firms, including Yankelovich Clancy Shulman, the Gallup organization, Cambridge Reports/Research International, the Hartman Group, and Roper's, have all grappled with the implications of greening for marketers in this period and often ended up portraying very different green-market scenarios.

While one 1991 survey found that 78 percent of Americans regularly declare themselves to be "environmentalists," for example, only 22 percent of those polled in another survey said they were "very often influenced in a buying decision" by environmental claims, and only 50 percent questioned in yet another survey indicated they had ever taken any actions on behalf of the environment—including, presumably, buying greener products.

One international survey found consumers around the world willing to pay higher prices for goods if these added costs meant less destruction of planet earth, but a similar study in the United States refined this finding to a willingness to pay only "a little more." Just one-quarter of consumers approached by one polling organization said they would buy from firms whose products they believed added to the pollution pool. Another survey, meanwhile, found that only 13 percent of respondents thought the environmental information provided by product-sellers was accurate—which makes one wonder how most people reach a decision about whether a company's products pollute in the first place, if almost no one believes the information about pollution coming from manufacturers.

Such confusing, sometimes contradictory opinions and numbers cause problems for professional marketers. But from the enomic standpoint, they nonetheless illustrate the growing importance of environmental concerns *generally* when it comes to product selling. And when one goes beyond very broad overviews and looks at how the environmental factor is affecting selling in some key demographic portions of the marketplace, its importance becomes even more apparent.

A product's perceived greenness, its earth-friendliness, tends to be of much greater concern to upscale and better-educated people living in the suburbs than to poorer urban and rural consumers. To selling professionals, this is a harbinger of things to come among all product buyers.

Automobiles, after all, were just playthings of the very rich before average Americans could afford to buy them. Televisions, when they were first sold commercially, cost the equivalent of several months' wages for most working people.

If the well-to-do end of the market is today moving in a green direction, clearly that is where the entire market is headed in years to come. Some confirmation of this view was found in still another study, which concluded that while 22 million Americans, most of them highly educated and well-to-do, were very prone to buy products perceived to be environmentally benign in 1990, this number was expected to reach 55 million by 1995, via a kind of trickling down of green preferences from consumer pace-setters to others who ultimately follow their purchasing lead.

A strong generational bias among the young when it comes to buying greener products is likewise not merely a sign of youthful fadism but another trend whose importance will only increase with the passage of time. Anyone who has spoken recently to a kid in kindergarten, a proto-adult in high school, or a member of any age group in between knows that environmental considerations often take on an almost religious fervor with youth.

Doubters need only do something as simple as throw a candy wrapper into the street in the presence of a grade schooler, instead of into a waste receptacle, to check the validity of this observation. The sheer wealth of knowledge about ecosystems and their problems possessed by the average American school child is, in the vernacular of the breed, awesome.

Environmental enthusiasts may attribute these changed attitudes to the worldwide emergence of a new earth-oriented consciousness. Conspiracy theorists may put them down to the endless propaganda efforts of the Elders of Gaia, six old crones operating out of a basement in Pasadena, California, who control Americans' thinking through dominance of the media— or perhaps via microwave emissions.

To marketers, it matters not a whit what generates such attitudes. The cause here is less important than its consequences. Today's young are tomorrow's buyers. If these people are increasingly enamored with a product's environmental soundness, for whatever reason, well . . .

Beyond income or generational predilections, still another way to approach the phenomenon of green goods selling is to view it within a larger aesthetic context. Everywhere one looks today, the consuming public is moving away from shop-till-you-drop thinking and acquisition-for-its-own-sake, and toward leaner, less "heavy" consuming preferences.

American shoppers do not want less. They want more *and* less. Or to put this another way, they want to get more out of less.

They want to ingest less food but derive more flavor and nutrition from what is eaten. They want more taste in their beverages, but with less bloated after-feelings. They may accept (grudgingly) the need for fewer sex partners as a matter of contemporary defensive health practices, but want to enjoy more intense and fulfilling sexual pleasures with these fewer partners.

The greener aspects of this new consumption aesthetic are likewise appearing everywhere: in the contents of goods from food to clothing; in their packaging; in the perceived overall sensitivity of product makers and sellers to the earth.

Finally, when it comes to generalizations about contemporary enomic marketing, it should be noted that almost no one actually *opposes* this changed way of making and selling. The primary obstructions to more rapid changes in this end of the economy are less based on outright opposition than linked to defining what terms such as environmentally sound and environmentally responsible actually mean, and in reconciling ecological imperatives with other desirable product characteristics.

The extraordinary difficulties inherent in defining what is, and what is not, ecologically correct have led the Federal Trade Commission to issue a green marketing guide, following complaints by attorneys general of eleven states about deceptive advertising on this subject. Several states (including traditional national pace-setters California and New York) have felt impelled to pass laws concerning the use of certain environmental terms manufacturers sometimes put on their labels.

At the trade group level, the Advertising Age Environmental Marketing and Advertising Council has put out a list of guidelines for marketers. At the consumer end of the market, these difficulties have led to the creation of two privately operated labeling programs, Green Seal and Green Cross, patterned along lines similar to successful programs inaugurated in West Germany as early as 1978, in Canada and Japan by 1988, and today in place in more than twenty nations around the world. The U.S. Environmental Protection Agency has got into the act with its own Energy Star certification program.

Still, after all these efforts, many consumers and manufacturers remain confused or even at loggerheads about which products do or do not hurt the earth. This confusion and disagreement, rather than resistance from some group or special interest, is impeding the spread of certain types of green marketing.

The second primary obstruction here involves the other

goals that occasionally conflict with a product's environmental soundness. Harried working parents, for example, may find extra packaging that contributes to solid waste buildup also makes it more convenient for them to turn out quick after-work microwave meals. Financially hard-pressed shoppers may buy the cheapest products, even if these incorporate some ecologically unsound contents. Merchants who may wish to improve their own reputations for being environmentally sensitive sometimes find that more elaborate packaging is still necessary to reduce theft in their stores.

Perhaps the most publicized example highlighting the conflict between going green in a mass market sense and opting for another priority involves disposable diapers. Some 17 billion of these baby aids are sold in the United States each year. Accordingly, throw-away diapers have long made up a significant share of this country's total solid waste stream.

At one time or another, twenty-two states have considered taxing this product as a means of getting parents to switch to less environmentally destructive washable cloth diapers. But no state has actually done so to date, and disposables still dominate in this area of baby care—though much less bulky, superabsorbent disposables from Kimberly-Clark and Proctor & Gamble are now starting to come to market.

Are losses on the diaper front a sign that green products are ephemeral in their appeal? Of course not. They merely signify that greenness is not the only thing shoppers consider when making a buying decision. No single product characteristic is ever the *only* thing shoppers consider when slapping down their money.

An environmentally sensitized economy does not mean that only "the environment" determines buying decisions any more than a car-based society means that no one walks from place to place, or even, on occasion, rides a horse.

Perhaps the best way to approach the pervasive but complex and often confusing elements of enomic marketing is to divide the subject into a product's own design or contents (what's in the box), a product's packaging (the box itself), and product selling per se (getting the box and its contents off the retailer's shelf and into the trunk of a consumer's car). What follows is a very abbreviated look at how this process is being played out in a few major markets.

When it comes to product contents and the new environmental economics, first came phosphates. During the 1970s, there emerged in this country a realization that excess amounts of phosphates found in laundry detergents, which ended up in inland waterways, were "killing" lakes by promoting growth of algae that consumed oxygen needed to sustain other aquatic species.

The upshot, after much bad press and other public pressure on manufacturers, was the introduction of phosphate-free laundry detergents. Ecologically, this proved a boon to fish. Economically, it also demonstrated something quite important to both product makers and consumers: Going green need mean no lasting penalty, either in terms of price or quality.

After phosphate-free detergents began being made by the truckload, they cost no more to manufacture and no more to buy. This helped dispel the notion on the product front that saving the world (or parts thereof) was necessarily a costly business for manufacturers or consumers.

In terms of quality, the lesson was equally profound. It might be summed up as the realization that simple cleanliness, in certain circumstances, might actually be preferable to "whiter-than-white" cleanliness. Once a large segment of the American public became willing to accept clothes that were merely clean, rather than glistening and eye-achingly clean, phosphates became just another option, not a necessity.

This was a relatively painless enomic transformation for all concerned. Manufacturers expanded their product lines. Consumers ended up with a more varied choice of products to accommodate their broadening tastes.

A situation that has yet to reach a similarly satisfactory resolution involves mutually acceptable standards for defining terms such as earth-friendly or green or natural or ozone-friendly or recycled when it comes to product content or design. The biodegradability dispute as applied to trash bags highlights difficulties here.

Makers of Hefty Trash Bags contended that their product broke down naturally over time and was therefore ecologically sound. This was challenged by some environmentalists, who said such biodegradation occurred only in sunlight, and not in conditions actually found in landfills where discarded products are buried and not subject to sunlight.

Biodegradability claims by Hefty were subsequently withdrawn. Many other product makers, concerned about challenges to their own green labeling, took the hint and stopped marketing programs based on environmental claims.

In certain cases, government pressure expedited these actions. In 1992, for example, the Federal Trade Commission challenged General Electric's energy-saving claims for its "Energy Choice" light bulbs because these products used less wattage largely by virtue of providing less light.

Such occurrences are noteworthy because they suggest the gradual learning process required by both manufacturers and consumers to achieve a fully enomic system of marketing. They did not signal a slowing in the transition to greener goods marketed in a greener manner. They were merely a sign that the gimmicky element of this process is coming to an end.

In understanding why so many product makers are today greening their wares, one critical factor is hard to exaggerate. This factor is the overall environmental exposure these manufacturers themselves face in producing goods.

Just as chemical, car, and computer chip makers have had to confront problems disposing of toxic materials at their factories, and have had to learn to be less wasteful of energy and raw materials in order to stay competitive, so too have makers of the countless mass-market products sold in supermarkets and discount stores. This necessity carries over naturally into the ecological impact of the goods sold by these same companies.

This is the "process thing" at work. If the way a company

manufactures is getting greener, it is virtually impossible for things the company manufactures not to become greener as well.

The contents and designs of so many products are today being influenced by new enomic imperatives, whether or not they are actually sold under a green banner, that it would be impossible to compile a comprehensive listing. Noting even a few current green (or greener) consumer items, however, suggests how widespread this phenomenon has become.

Parker Hannifin, a maker of pleasure craft, advertises the less-polluting "responsible boating" technology employed in its product line. Half a dozen leading coffee accessory suppliers now sell unbleached coffee filters, usually at premium prices. Church & Dwight, which markets Arm & Hammer products, has made its baking soda line virtually synonymous with "natural" cleaning. Rubbermaid offers an extensive group of household recycling products.

The Howard Corporation now offers a complete line of facial paper, towels, and napkins marketed under the ENVISION label. Many long-popular Marcal recycled products, meanwhile, are today being sold in ways that emphasize their recycled contents. The Scott Paper Company is selling a supersize roll of toilet tissue for public restrooms, reducing interior roll core waste with a bigger-is-better approach.

In the rag trades, organic cotton, raised without chemicals, is becoming widely available for would-be wearers of earth-friendly clothing. Nike, the sneaker giant, has a program to turn used sneakers into feedstock for the outsoles of its newer footwear. The list goes on and on.

Just as concern for the environment is bringing about basic changes in product content, it is doing the same when it comes to packaging. The debate here involves all manner of metal (mostly cans), plastic, and paper-cardboard packaging, with vendors of all these materials talking up the actual or potential recycling capabilities of their respective wares. Some paper-cardboard vendors add that their own offerings are renewable to boot.

With respect to paper goods, de-inking technologies are vastly better today than they were just a few years ago, providing a new quality argument to support greater use of recycled stock from newsprint. There is a fast-diminishing difference in the appearance of wrappings that contain higher percentages of recycled as against all-virgin stock. Even where quality differences continue to be significant, there is growing acceptance of higher recycled content in paper packaging by its end users.

In Europe, people have long accepted less whiteness in their paper because of economic considerations. Today's Americans are becoming more receptive to recycled stock largely because of environmental concerns. The analogy between this attitude change vis-à-vis paper and a willingness to accept something other than whiter-than-white in one's towels is of course obvious.

The internationalization of world markets is having its own effects when it comes to greener packaging in this country. Carmakers around the world are reducing emissions in order to meet tougher California regulations aimed at improving air quality, because California's market is so important in the overall car-selling equation. Similarly, new packaging laws coming into effect in consumer goods–hungry Germany are obliging American multinationals to hasten the greening of their packaging worldwide in order to market effectively in Central Europe.

An enomic version of Gresham's Law is apparent in all such situations. Just as bad money drives good money out of circulation, greener packaging in one key market tends to drive more polluting packaging out of all markets.

The many disagreements swirling around plastics are perhaps today's most high-profile environmental packaging issue. It is relatively easy for people to sort steel and aluminum cans for reclamation, which is why so many of both are recycled, and to do the same for containers made of clear and green glass, materials now recycled to the tune of about 20 percent. Hundreds of different plastics are used in everyday packaging, however, and sorting them for reuse is therefore a much tougher proposition.

These plastics can be divided into seven basic categories based on the resins used in their manufacture, which simplifies some recycling problems. But not all. Mixing plastics of different categories can ruin a recycling program.

The American Plastics Council (formerly the Partnership for Plastics Progress), an industry group, estimated that only about one-third of popular polythylene terephthalate (PET) plastics found in items such as large soda bottles were actually recycled in 1991. When all kinds of plastic packaging were considered, just 2.2 percent of the 6.7 million tons of plastic packaging were found to be recycled in 1990, and less than 5 percent were being recycled a year later.

Still, increasing, if not yet statistically overwhelming, amounts of plastic packaging are finding new commercial incarnations. Threats from at least thirty-five states to outlaw nonbiodegradable or recyclable plastics at some future date have encouraged industry efforts here.

Market researcher James D. Nail recently noted that half the plastic packaging in Proctor & Gamble's Downy fabric softener, a quarter of the plastics in ERA and Dash laundry detergent packages, and all the plastic in Spic and Span Pine liquid cleaner bottles are made from recycled stock. Heinz, not so long ago, replaced a multiplastic composite in its squeezable ketchup bottle with a more easily recycled PET plastic.

On a larger canvas, Proctor & Gamble's broad-based "Closing the Loop" program aims to create recycling infrastructure not only for PET but for multicolor high-density polyethylene (HDPE) plastics as well. A British manufacturer, Imperial Chemical Industries, introduced a shampoo line during the 1992 Earth Summit packaged in "natural" plastics derived from plant material, an innovation in plastics' content that, if pursued, could have a very big effect on the way plastics and compatibility with the environment are perceived.

Jacquelyn Ottman, a consultant on marketing and packaging issues, has examined the already highly articulated green strategies of scores of this country's leading consumer product makers. Her findings, presented in *Green Marketing: Challenges and Opportunities for the New Marketing Age* (1992),

amply demonstrate the burgeoning interest of America's leading firms in all such endeavors.

Ottman also notes a trend among some product manufacturers not just to reduce exterior packaging but to eliminate
some of it all together. By putting all the information a consumer needs to know on a tube of toothpaste, for example,
then standing that tube upright on its own enlarged flat cap,
instead of displaying this same information on a box or on a
"blister pack" for pegboard display, packaging waste reduction is realized without the necessity of recycling.

Such waste minimization at its source may well be the
enomic wave of the future for the $70 billion-a-year American
packaging industry. For the time being, the chasing-arrow recycling logo now found on so many product packages is a
ubiquitous sign that corporate America and environmentalist
America are steadily (if not yet systematically) healing their
long, deep rift over packaging.

Along with product content, along with product packaging, the third leg of this country's enomic marketing triad
involves the retailing function.

Earlier in this chapter, we note the occasional dichotomy
between retailing and environmental priorities. Retailers sometimes want more packaging to accommodate their customers'
desire for food that cooks and carries more easily, and the
retailers' own security requirements. (Bigger boxes are harder
to conceal and steal.)

But there is another side to both these selling priorities. It
is the side on which the environment and the selling function
complement one another rather than conflict.

When it comes to convenience, consider the absolute inanity (from a customer's standpoint) of buying anything but an
ultra-concentrated laundry detergent. You are coming home
from a murderous ten-hour day at the office. You have to stop
at the store to buy a dozen food and household items. You
have lower back pain, and face the prospect of cleaning a house
and cooking a dinner for a family as tired and stressed out as
yourself.

Do you, or any consumer in this all-too-common contemporary situation, really want to carry a sixty-four-ounce detergent container home, when all but eight of these ounces is water that could be added from a household tap? Or need not even be added at all, because when concentrate is dumped into a washer, the machine's own water creates a full-blown clothes cleaner?

Convenience packaging. Greener packaging. There is no difference here.

Such packaging helps explain why more than 55 percent of the laundry detergents sold in this country during a three-month period at the end of 1992, as tracked by Information Sources, Inc., were superconcentrates. The 21 million ton, $4 billion-a-year laundry detergent market, in fact, is coming to be dominated by enomically packaged products, to the delight not only of ecology-minded consumers but of manufacturers as well, who make a greater profit with this product line than from its more traditional predecessors.

In this same scenario, retailers not only serve their clientele better by stocking more lightly packaged items, they also improve their store's profitability through better space allocation. Concentrates take up less shelf space than water-bloated items, meaning there is more space for other items. So why not stock concentrates whenever possible?

With regard to security, the old idea that bigger product boxes are a necessity in helping to reduce theft is giving way to greater use of electronic theft-stoppers. These tag items with devices that sound an alarm when goods are leaving the store without benefit of sales slip. The result: better security and less environment-destroying packaging.

On the disposal front, the announcement by Sears in 1991 that it intended to cut its retail waste stream by 25 percent over five years was a simple acknowledgment that taking out the trash has become a costly business expense for retailers. American retailers are looking very carefully at the cost of commercial trash disposal, with an eye to cutting overhead whenever possible.

In what is perhaps an indication of what lies ahead when it comes to retail solid waste handling, Browning-Ferris Industries, the country's largest commercial trash collector, recently set up a recycling center in the basement of a huge retail mall in Minnesota. Bringing recycling closer to the source of trash in this way might prove quite effective for both retailers and collectors in years to come.

Projecting a more positive image factor, of course, is the most obvious benefit of selling green for many retailers. During the 1980s, mail-order catalog sellers of "environmental products" such as Seventh Generation, Co-Op America, We Care, and Real Good News, along with organizational sellers of similar products such as the Sierra Club and Greenpeace, and store-based environmental specialty retailers such as The Body Shop, proved the enormous potential of the environmental market niche.

In the present decade, more traditional retailers are moving to get a piece of this action with environmental "concept" departments in their discount and department outlets. And making sure they do not offend the pervasive pro-environmental sensibilities of their customers generally. And reducing their waste-handling overhead. And, on occasion, where items containing tomorrow's equivalent of asbestos and lead paint may be on the shelves, reducing their litigation exposure as well.

Thus, while mega-retailer Sears moves to reduce its solid waste stream, mega-retailer Wal-Mart plans to open a prototype outlet in Lawrence, Kansas, that will feature a variety of environmentally sound innovations ranging from solar-powered signs, to collection bins for waste wrapping, to classrooms where ecology subjects can be taught to shopper-visitors.

On the comestible front, with the United States now home to more than 11 million people who call themselves vegetarians, the multibillion-dollar organic food retailing business, in both conventional and specialty outlets, continues to grow rapidly. "Earth-friendly picnics" built around appropriate foods and recyclable or biodegradable eating implements flourish. And chefs in leading restaurants around the country move to green their kitchens by buying organically grown vegetables, "recycling" untouched leftovers for the needy through organizations like City Harvest, Inc. in New York and sending formerly trashed food waste out for composting.

It is the greening of McDonald's, however, that really catches the eye of people seeking portents of how the environment is likely to restructure America's popular eating habits in years to come. In 1991 the McDonald's Corporation, which serves 22 million people a day, began working with the Environmental Defense Fund on ways to reduce the solid waste impact of its polystyrene "clamshell" food containers, and on other food and packaging issues.

The result of this eight-month joint effort was a forty-two-point program McDonald's hopes will eventually cut its solid waste output by 80 percent, replace much traditional waste disposal with ecofriendly composting, and increase the percentage of recycled paper and cardboard used in its carry-out bags and corrugated delivery boxes. The company also has announced plans to build at least one of its new outlets largely out of recycled materials.

Greener product making, packaging, and retailing of everything from soft goods to fast foods fit easily into a larger, evolving enomic context. The marketing function must be rationalized and made more efficient, in exactly the same way as the manufacturing and transportation functions must be rationalized and rendered more efficient. Stiffer competition, new consumer preferences, avoiding down-the-road environmental litigation liabilities: All make these actions a necessity for consumer product makers and sellers, just as they do for other businesses.

Taking an even broader view, one quickly sees that a more enomic mode of marketing all kinds of goods is absolutely inevitable because of other trends noted throughout these pages. How can manufacturers not continue to green their products' content at a time when the strain on water systems, and costs to society of protecting these systems, is soaring? How can manufacturers not dramatically reduce packaging volume when the monetary and aesthetic costs of trash proliferation are exploding, and packaging accounts for 30 percent of America's municipal waste stream?

In the 1970s, green marketing was an ideological totem. Now and into the foreseeable future, it is a core component of getting the goods out the door and the cash into the register.

SIX

THE GREEN TRADES

When most people think of the greening of the U.S. economy, they think in terms of companies that provide environmental services or sell pollution control equipment—companies identified with the "green trades." Such a view, of course, as noted throughout these pages, is far, far too restrictive.

Every major sector of the U.S. economy, every manufacturing and marketing component, is today undergoing an environmental restructuring aimed at making it more efficient and less wasteful, less prone to cleanup liabilities in years to come, and better able to tap burgeoning consumer demand for greener products and services. This is what the new environmental economics is all about. This is the core reality of enomics.

The environmental services, pollution control industry is merely one of the more obvious beneficiaries of this vast restructuring. It is very far from being the drama's main event.

Indeed, on the broad canvas, environmental cleanup can be viewed as a temporary economic phenomenon. Once enough companies in other economic sectors become truly efficient, and either learn how to produce without releasing toxic materials into the environment or how to recycle these materials completely, the amount of toxics handled by the green trades will decline automatically.

The same can be said about the nontoxic solid waste (trash) currently produced by cities and private companies. Once enough of this material is properly recycled and returned to the manufacturing loop or turned into compost that is used in various agricultural applications, this end of the environmental cleanup business will shrink as well.

For the time being, however, and for some time to come, in this country and around the world, the economic importance of the green trades will be quite significant. Their present and near-term dimensions are therefore worth discussing at some length.

As noted elsewhere, at least $100 billion is spent by industry and another $30 billion or so by government in the United States on various forms of waste handling and pollution prevention. Together, these sums were the equivalent of about 2 percent of this country's gross national product (GNP) in 1990. By 1996, approximately $175 billion is expected to be spent on environmental cleanup; and in the year 2000, when more than $260 billion in such spending is projected, this sum will equal some 3 percent of the GNP.

The generic aims of these activities are to protect the natural environment, protect the health and safety of people, and remove or "neutralize" aesthetically unpleasant sights and smells related to industrial and agricultural processes. Some 65,000 to 70,000 American firms specialize in these fields today. In addition, innumerable companies have divisions active in the green trades, often to handle cleanup projects for other divisions within their own corporate families.

The environmental cleanup work performed by all these entities can be broken down into four basic categories: air pollution control, hazardous waste management, solid (nonhazardous) waste management, and water and wastewater treatment.

Solid waste management generates some $27 billion in revenues annually, and when recycling and industrial resource recovery is included, more than $45 billion in revenues. Water treatment, related equipment sales, and spending by private water utilities in this country's 15,500 municipalities account for another $25 to $30 billion in revenues. Hazardous waste management and air pollution control each generate more than $15 billion in revenues.

These four basic groups are sometimes further broken down according to the kinds of work done by waste handlers. Such work includes monitoring, engineering, consulting, and laboratory analysis. Such specialty functions themselves generate considerable business. Environmental consulting, for example, produced between $8 and $10 billion in revenues for several hundred American engineering firms in 1991.

A number of additional categories, including so-called industrial services (plant maintenance, hydroblasting, and so on), which work to preserve environmental quality in the workplace, are sometimes considered to be part of the overall environmental cleanup business too. Such inclusions help explain why some experts see the private end of this industry as a $100 billion-a-year business, others put the figure at $120 billion a year, and still others peg it at $140 billion a year or higher.

Another way to view and categorize the environmental cleanup industry is to look beyond function to the specific type of waste handled. Hazardous waste management, for example, not only encompasses engineering, consulting, analysis, and remediation functions, but applies these functions to problems such as nuclear waste processing, dioxin control, "red-bag" waste disposal, and electric arc dust recycling of zinc.

These problem-solving specialties, in turn, tend to be closely linked to operations of specific sectors of the U.S. economy. Nuclear waste processing is an issue that mostly affects the electric utility industry. Dioxins are a by-product of timber mill operations. Zinc dust is produced by steel manufacturers.

Red-bag materials—used hypodermic needles, blood-soaked bandages and isotopes—are by-products of the health care establishment. More than 260,000 tons of this red-bag material was generated in 1990 (about 80 percent by hospitals), and more than 450,000 tons is expected to be generated by the year 2000.

As this brief sketch of the environmental industry suggests, this sector of the U.S. economy is now highly articulated, organized, and diversified. Certainly, it has its own not-yet-fully-tapped specialty niches, its venture capital-oriented situations, and its many unique entrepreneurial opportunities (which are treated at some length in Chapter 6). But people still mired in the notion that the environmental industry is in any sense a start-up or peripheral economic activity are decades off the mark.

Since 1970, the green trades have blossomed in this country as few other industries have blossomed. During the 1980s it was not uncommon for companies in this field to enjoy regular annual growth rates of 20 or 30 percent. In train with this growth came profound changes in the industry's image and management practices, especially in the realms of solid and hazardous waste handling, which together account for the bulk of environmental cleanup revenues.

To be sure, operating garbage trucks still does not attract Ivy Leaguers intent on ministering to the needs of Mother Gaia in a conspicuously down-to-earth fashion. Nonetheless, the people most closely identified with waste handling in the United States today are a very different breed from what was commonplace before 1970.

The evolution of management styles within the environmental cleanup industry in many ways mimics what occurred during a comparable period in the gambling industry. As legal gambling spread around this country, as state lotteries replaced numbers running, as legal gaming palaces replaced (at least partially) basement craps-shooting emporia, a pronounced and highly visible mob presence gradually succumbed to, or was subordinated by, more standard American corporate practices.

Unsavory elements continue to have a presence in gaming. The same is true in the green trades. But in both instances, to an ever-diminishing extent.

Wall Street oversight of publicly owned companies, government regulation, plus the high-teching of many waste handling and disposal functions, which has brought thousands of highly educated, highly reputable people into the field, have all worked to create far more responsible and aboveboard operations than existed in the green trades just a few years back.

A business demimonde has been largely assimilated into the corporate mainstream. Practices such as midnight dumping in pristine forests of fifty-five gallon drums filled with toxic materials are on the wane, if not quite totally a thing of the past. Even mixing "slightly" toxic wastes with city trash that eventually ends up being buried in ordinary landfills is on the decline.

There are still some nasty exceptions to this industry transformation, of course. New York City's $2 billion-a-year hauling business continues to be notorious for practices that cost commercial waste-generators hundreds of millions of dollars annually for "services" that often amount to little more than protection payoffs. Within the building trades in many parts of the country, too, a practice known as short-dumping (carting construction wastes to urban lots rather than all the way to landfills) is still quite prevalent, as more and more construction waste is classified "toxic," thereby boosting its disposal cost and adding incentives to circumvent the law.

But even these nasty carry-overs are fading. Competition, increased recycling, and a new law in New York City that regulates how much can be charged per cubic yard of commercial waste are all working to lessen the influence of corrupt haulers in the city. Short-dumping, too, has become a special object of regulatory enforcement in cities around the country.

Viewing the overall corporate image cleansing taking place within the green trades, one is reminded of the remark made by the Meyer Lansky–like character in the second *Godfather* movie. Speaking to the Corleone heir-apparent, he said: "Michael. We're 90 percent legitimate now. And we're bigger than General Motors." This pretty well sums up the ongoing evolution of management style within the American waste-handling industry.

*   *   *

At the start of the 1990s, stock analysts expected both revenues and profitability in waste handling to continue growing, as they had all during the 1980s. The theory here was that unlike the generic greening of the United States and world economies described elsewhere in this book, which is largely a market-based phenomenon tied to new efficiency imperatives and consumer tastes, the environmental cleanup industry itself was "regulation-driven" and therefore recession-proof.

Tougher and tougher environmental laws are being passed all the time, ran this thinking. The EPA alone now has more than nine thousand environmental regulations. More and more money would thus inevitably continue to be transferred from polluters to pollution cleaner-uppers.

Alas, there were several defects in this prognostication. The most significant arose from the fact that the green trades, the environmental cleanup industry, turned out to be every bit as responsive to changing market forces as to government regulations.

With everyone expecting ever-higher prices to be paid collectors and disposers of trash, excess handling capacities developed. This occurred at the same time that municipal recycling programs were reducing stocks of city-generated trash requiring landfilling, and a recession was cutting into the 40 percent of the solid waste business accounted for by servicing commercial clients.

The result was much stiffer competition within the $27 billion-a-year (exclusive of its recycling component) solid waste management field. The pace of consolidation in this end of the environmental cleanup industry also quickened as margins flattened during the late 1980s. Weak players went under. The toll was especially high among small, independent ma-and-pa suburban trash-collecting operators.

Technology played its own role in this competitive process. Companies that run this country's 135 trash-to-steam plants have been garnering ever-larger shares of trash in recent years, adding to competitive pressures on solid waste buriers. In 1990 incinerators collected 25 million tons of available trash stocks; they are expected to collect twice that amount by the year 2000.

Buriers, for their part, collected about 130 million tons in 1990 but are expected to collect only about 95 million tons by the year 2000. This reduced tonnage will have to be dumped in larger, more ecologically secure, and therefore more expensive-to-operate regional landfills, which will replace the 5,500 widely dispersed, mostly low-tech landfills that currently dot the American landscape.

High-teching of these new facilities will not only include elaborate precautions to prevent seepage of waste into groundwater but perhaps plasma-arc burning of some garbage as well. The plasma-arc disposal method, already used extensively in parts of Europe and Asia, burns landfill garbage at such high temperatures that it turns to glass. In this way more trash is permanently "fused" into less space.

All these kinds of advanced technology, of course, are too expensive for the smallish concerns that used to predominate in the solid waste business. New technologies becoming available in this field increasingly favor players with deeper pockets.

As important as market forces such as competition, recession, and technology are to fortunes of firms in the solid waste business are the environmental liabilities faced by these same companies. Regulations, it turns out, can limit profits even as they boost revenues.

Most people think this rule applies only to hazardous waste handling facilities, which, as noted above, resemble nuclear power plants. They are cash cows during years they actually operate. Then comes the nasty expense of permanently closing them down, and cash cows suddenly turn into white elephants.

Because people in the business of collecting and disposing of other people's toxic wastes are also taking on all the liabilities that come with this material, it is perfectly natural that an old toxic waste handling facility should end up in a Superfund site. A fair number of the 1,275 sites on the Superfund National Priority List in mid-1992, and many more in the Comprehensive Environmental Response, Compensation and Liability Information System's own much larger 36,000-site registry, fit this description.

To a distressing degree, sites long used to bury so-called *non*hazardous wastes (garbage landfills) are likewise becoming white elephants. Quite a number of these facilities are now generating liability surprises for their municipal and corporate owners.

Burning rather than burying wastes tends to do away with liabilities associated with soil and water contamination. But burning creates air pollution problems, which require costly outlays to address. Operators of this country's sixty large-scale toxic waste incinerating facilities, who garner $2.5 billion in revenues annually for performing this function, have had ample opportunities to discover this fact in recent years.

Along with competitive and liability problems, solid waste handlers face additional difficulties involving antitrust laws, increasingly heavy fines that are integral to their core business activities, and threatened restrictions on interstate trash hauling. And then, of course, there are those special industry bugaboos, NIMBY and BANANA.

These acronyms are used to sum up the ever-present frustrations faced by all waste handlers in siting new facilities. In the good old days, when things were merely very hard, NIMBY (Not In My Back Yard) was the usual attitude of the general public in this regard. Now things have gotten *really* tough and gone BANANA (Build Absolutely Nothing Anywhere Near Anyone).

With all the problems and frustrations, 1991 was nonetheless a relatively good year for most solid waste, hazardous waste, air pollution control, and water treatment environmental companies. According to the *Environmental Industry Yearbook & Investment Guide*, average revenues reported by this country's seventy largest such environmental firms rose about 18 percent, down a bit from previous years but still quite respectable.

Even average net incomes (bottom lines) of these companies were up modestly that year, while their employment managed a 4 percent increase—paltry by previous standards, but rather impressive compared to the job-downscaling mania sweeping industries such as retailing, automaking, and computers in 1991.

In 1992, however, the recession finally hit the environmental industry with full force. Revenue growth, particularly of companies handling industrial wastes generated by the nation's slumping manufacturers, grew at a slack pace or were actually flat. Stiff competition, more costly regulations as they affected cleaner-uppers themselves, and the many other factors noted earlier all combined to hurt bottom lines.

Clearly, the 1990s are emerging as a shakeout period for the green trades. Even a new Clinton administration, more favorably disposed to environmental cleanup, will not change this fact. Until the effects of waste minimization and recycling fully permeate the American economy, however, this industry's revenues and importance (if not its profits) will continue to grow.

Jobs, and worries about not having one, were the defining issue of the presidential campaign that brought Bill Clinton to the White House. A prominent feature of that campaign was a discussion of how many jobs would be created cleaning up the environmental mess in this country and how many would be destroyed in the process.

In a very fundamental sense, of course, the argument about jobs and the environment, as it was framed during the 1992 election season, was absurd. As Susan Cohn points out in her book *Green At Work* (1992), the real employment issue here involves a changed viewpoint, a new set of skills needed by increasing numbers of people in *all* kinds of industries and professions, not growth of a few distinct work classifications.

Cohn believes that American business generally is facing environment-linked challenges that employees generally must help to meet. The skills to do this are an ability to look from "the inside" at a company's operations, see how they are being threatened by environmental exposure, and reduce this exposure by helping change the way the firm operates. Doing this also involves looking from "the inside" to see how new green marketing opportunities can best be exploited.

Cohn writes less of environmental employment per se than of environmental literacy as a generic requisite for many (if not most) jobs in a greening economy. Rather like computer literacy. Or just plain literacy, for that matter.

This is almost certainly the most intelligent way to approach "environmental employment." But not surprisingly, it being American politics, this was not the perspective adopted during the 1992 campaign.

There, the Bush forces spoke of 32,000 logging jobs that would be lost in northwestern states if proposed programs to save the spotted owl were carried out and 300,000 autoworker jobs that could be lost in the upper Midwest if tougher corporate average fuel efficiency (CAFE) standards were enacted.

The Clinton organization responded by citing estimates that as many as 2 million Americans now earn their livelihoods doing some kind of environmental cleanup work, of which approximately 850,000 are employed by private companies in the green trades. Domestic payrolls of just the largest forty such companies grew between 1990 and 1991 from 134,800 to 146,400. Another million or so Americans, according to the Clinton campaign, do environmental work for government, nonprofit institutions, or hold in-house corporate cleanup jobs.

The perspective expressed throughout this book is much closer to Cohn's view that all jobs are more or less obliged to take on a greener tinge in a greening economy, than to that of either candidate in the last presidential campaign. Pursuing this perspective when it comes to the green trades, specific job numbers (which the Bureau of Labor Statistics' standard industrial codes do not provide in any case) are less informative than considering the process by which employment generally is going green.

There is a *life-cycle pattern* in green employment growth. To understand this pattern is to understand the gradual integration of environment-linked factors into the muscle and fiber of the entire American economic system. It is to sense how the reality of employment within a single economic sector, the green trades, and the concept of environmental literacy throughout the entire economy, are gradually coming together.

Between 1970 and 1980, when the first incarnations of all key federal environmental laws were being written, and complementary statutes were starting to appear at the state and local levels, environmental employment consisted mostly of government work. Working green meant signing on to write rules and regs for the EPA and its lesser bureaucratic clones.

From 1980 through about 1985, with many environmental laws already on the books, the country set out to discover just how bad pollution damages of various kinds really were. During these years the "white smock technologists" came into their own. Monitoring and testing became the main growth area in environmental employment.

Since the mid-1980s, spending on both actual cleanup projects and environmentally streamlining corporate operations have started in earnest. This has created hard-hat environmental infrastructure construction jobs, design and engineering jobs, compliance jobs within corporations, and much-expanded opportunities for ecoentrepreneurs.

Since the early 1990s, there also has been a very dramatic increase in environment management programs taught at business schools. In 1992 alone, such programs were instituted or much expanded at such prestigious institutions as Harvard, Yale, and the Massachusetts Institute of Technology, while continuing environmental management education programs similar to those instituted at New York University in 1991 also spread around the country. Literally hundreds of corporate in-house and trade group management programs, mostly built around compliance training, are now in place as well.

The growing edge when it comes to environmental employment in the 1990s, as exemplified by this new management training, is thus *not* in special green job categories. It is to be found in "standard" employment going green. This trend is yet another symptom of the growing mainstream nature of a new environmental economics.

*   *   *

No discussion of the green trades can fail to emphasize the importance of recycling. While the answer to many of this country's most pressing ecological and economic problems *ultimately* lies in reducing the volume of waste produced throughout the production-distribution-consumption cycle, recycling provides a necessary temporary solution to many of these problems.

Recycling activities are thus critical in helping to bring into being a rationalized, superefficient economic system that replicates nature in making endless and unlimited consumption possible without resource depletion. These activities have arguably also become this country's fastest-growing and most dynamic set of enterprises.

From the point of view of traditional, large-scale waste handling, recycling did not begin entering the economic mainstream (at least in peacetime) before the 1960s. A professional recycler prior to this time was likely to spend his workdays seated on a beach chair next to a trailer in company with a large dog of questionable pedigree surrounded by partially dismembered vehicles. Along with car parts, the only significant recycling activities in those days were built around scrap metals such as copper, paper, and perhaps glass.

Initially, after the first Earth Day in 1970, environmentalists viewed recycling as the alternative to burying or incinerating wastes. Gradually this outlook changed. By the time the 1990s rolled around, recycling had become an important part of virtually all conventional waste-handling operations.

Today a modern waste management facility cannot be run without a recycling component. The reason is largely nitty-gritty economics. It costs a lot of money to get permits for a waste facility, and the return on this investment depends to a great extent on how long the facility can operate.

If a landfill's capacity is 1,000 units, if it accepts 100 units per year, none of which is recycled, the landfill can stay open for 10 years. If 20 of these units are recycled annually, the landfill can stay open 12 years. If 50 units are recycled annually, the landfill can stay open 15 years. Nitty-gritty economics.

The extraordinarily pervasive quality of present-day recycling throughout the U.S. economy is most readily understood when one looks at the different terms used to describe this activity in different economic contexts. When materials are salvaged from ordinary municipal trash, curbside recycling is the term of choice; from manufacturing or industrial waste streams (sometimes using very advanced technologies), the process is called resource recovery; when recycling involves farm or forest materials, it is composting; when heat energy is being collected and recycled, it is known as cogeneration.

Curbside recycling has been enormously successful in this country in terms of segregating out materials that can be plowed back into the productive mainstream. More than 4,000 curbside programs serving 70 million Americans now operate in U.S. cities and towns.

Recycling of beer and soft drink containers increased almost 750 percent between 1972 and 1987, and recycling of food packaging increased some 200 percent in this same period. The amount of old newspapers collected for recycling jumped 90 percent between 1983 and 1991. In all, according to the EPA, 17 percent of America's annually generated trash was being recycled by 1990, compared to just 7 percent two decades earlier. Some 25 percent is projected by the end of this decade.

Unfortunately, because the infrastructure to turn materials back into new products has evolved more slowly than the collection process, much potentially recyclable material now ends up being sent to landfills anyway. In 1991, a city like Philadelphia was sorting about 12 percent of its trash for recycling but recycling only 5 percent. The rest ended up being deposited in landfills.

New York City in 1991 recycled 12 percent of its trash and plans to recycle more than 40 percent by the year 2000. It was so swamped with collections by 1992, however, it was only able to recycle about 1,000 tons a day, rather than the 2,100 tons mandated by the city's own ordinances.

Institutional solutions to the current bottlenecks afflicting "feedstock" generated by curbside recycling are rapidly coming into place, however. Ten states already have laws requiring local newspapers to use recycled paper, for example, thus boosting demand for this material. More than 31 million tons of newprint were recycled or exported in 1991, up from 26.4 million tons three years earlier, according to the American Paper Institute.

It seems safe to say that when adequate infrastructure is finally in place, the problem of too many curbside recyclables being collected will no longer exist. An end to recessionary times will likewise help reduce current surpluses more quickly.

The old saying "One man's meat is another man's poison" is a neat way of summing up what is happening with much of this country's former *industrial* waste. Literally thousands of purchases are being made today of discarded industrial metals, sludges, acid, solvents, and other environmentally destructive materials, by companies that regard this waste as raw materials for their own businesses.

Indeed, a community of middlemen brokering such deals has come into being in recent years. By 1990, the exchanges they operate were handling 7.9 million metric tons of industrial wastes. These exchanges help their suppliers save on disposal costs and their customers save on costs of virgin stocks.

A much greater amount of industrial waste is being recycled in-house by companies practicing resource recovery. Even during a recession, when raw material costs remain relatively low, costly disposal regulations make it worthwhile for more and more firms to retain "waste" within their own manufacturing loops.

The creation in August 1992 of the Buy-Recycled Business Alliance is emblematic of the serious attention big American business now pays to recycling. This alliance, which includes some of this country's largest firms in the chemical, retailing, fast-food, beverage, publishing, aluminum, and banking industries, purchased an estimated $2.7 billion worth of recycled materials in 1992.

Green trade firms that help high-polluting manufacturing firms meet tough new environmental laws through recycling instead of disposal are appearing everywhere. One of the better known and more successful is Horsehead Resource Development in Palmerton, Pennsylvania. Its core business involves recycling the zinc calcine found in hazardous dust produced by electric arc furnaces. Tough EPA regulations applicable to this dust, plus a market for recovered zinc, work to make a business like this one sustainable.

Composting is a term used to describe something that people do consciously with organic wastes that nature has always done with similar materials to keep them from becoming waste. If you leave organic material in a pile, it ultimately breaks down and becomes new environmental building blocks.

Individual farmers and gardeners by the millions have long engaged in composting. Now so do a goodly number of American cities and counties on a far grander scale.

A survey by *Biocycle Magazine* found 149 sludge ("biosolids") composting facilities operating in this country by the end of 1991, with another 126 in various stages of development. Most are part of urban water treatment programs. A few of these produce fertilizer by-products that are sold commercially in lawn and garden supply stores.

Biocycle also found that more than 2,200 yard-waste composting sites now service 18.5 million people in the seventeen states that responded to another of its surveys. Overall, according to the *Wall Street Journal*, by 1991 an estimated 12 percent of the yard waste in this country was being composted.

At municipal landfills around the country, some waste is being composted, some recycled, and some buried or incinerated. At a few of these landfills, the methane released when trash decomposes is burned to generate electricity—an interesting technological mix of composting and incineration.

Before leaving the green trades dedicated to environmental cleanup and turning in Chapter 6 to another group of firms cashing in on greener consumer tastes through entrepreneurial enterprises, one other important characteristic of the U.S. waste-handling business should be noted—its increasingly international character.

Government and business spending on environmental

protection and restoration in this country is greater than anywhere else in the world. It will total between $1.2 and $1.5 trillion during this decade, according to government estimates, while worldwide such spending will total between $3 and $4 trillion.

Naturally, with such sums up for grabs, businesspeople in the U.S. green trades are seeking not only to secure their places in the domestic environmental marketplace but to get pieces of the foreign action. Foreign businesspeople also are looking to capture as large a share of the enormous U.S. environmental cleanup marketplace as their capital resources and technologies allow.

The extent to which U.S. environmental firms have taken advantage of foreign green business opportunities can be seen in a quick reading of the annual reports and 10-Ks (reports prepared for the Securities and Exchange Commission) of virtually any leading player in this field. The best-known example here is Waste Management, Inc., and its still largely company-owned Waste Management International (WMI) spin-off. Today WMI is one of the most important waste-handling entities in Europe, with sales that grew 31 percent in 1991 to $1.1 billion.

Other examples of U.S. green companies penetrating overseas environmental markets include a large-scale joint venture in Japanese waste-to-steam projects by Wheelabrator Technologies, Roy F. Weston, Inc.'s West European environmental engineering joint venture with an Irish firm, Pacific Nuclear's move into nuclear waste handling outside the United States, Isco's water-monitoring product sales in countries around the world, ICF's burgeoning Pacific Rim environmental business, Safety-Kleen's solvent recycling operations in the United Kingdom, and activated carbon maker Calgon Carbon's increased activities in Japan and other Pacific markets.

Such examples, of course, are merely suggestive. A great many other U.S.-based environmental cleanup companies have penetrated foreign markets.

Selling American green goods (environmental services and pollution control equipment) abroad is, in fact, already a major element of the United States' international trade picture. Such trade, in turn, is of increasing relevance to this country's overall economic well-being, as we move from a domestic-oriented economy to one far more integrated into a larger international economic order. Just between 1986 and 1992, exports of American-made manufactured goods jumped 90 percent. Without this increase, the nation's recession would have been much deeper.

In a report prepared by the International Trade Administration of the U.S. Department of Commerce, it was estimated that by 1990, though most green goods were still being produced domestically by the world's polluting nations, as much as $50 *billion* worth of these services and equipment were being traded among nations. American firms, stated this report, were getting a hefty $3–$6 billion worth of this annual international commerce.

Even in the short time since that report was issued, there has been an enormous jump in actual or proposed environmental spending around the world. Taiwan's multibillion-dollar national infrastructure upgrade during the 1990s, with its huge environment-related component, is one part of this international increase.

So, too, is the plan announced by Mexico in 1992 to spend $4 billion on air pollution control and increase its overall environmental spending by 27 percent in 1993. The World Bank gave substance to the air cleanup part of this program by approving a $228 million loan to Mexico for this purpose in late 1992.

Countries such as Spain, which is vying for a place under the European Community (EC) economic umbrella, are boosting environmental spending sharply. Germany and other EC nations are doing the same. Environmental spending in nations of the old Soviet Bloc is going up—albeit slowly, because of economic difficulties related to the fall of communism. Environmental spending in the ABC countries of Latin America (Argentina, Brazil, and Chile) is also rising.

The $3 trillion to $4 trillion cited earlier as an estimate of total worldwide spending on environmental cleanup during the 1990s may thus well turn out to be an underestimate. And quite possibly, a massive one.

The congressional Office of Technology Assessment in 1992 projected that worldwide environmental cleanup expenditures would "soon" reach $300 billion per annum. A projection by the *Environmental Business Journal* that same year, however, estimated that worldwide green spending had already reached $270 billion by 1991 and would surpass $400 billion by 1996.

Almost every prediction made about national or international cost of environmental cleanup in decades past, in fact, has turned out to be far too conservative. That was the case when West Germany absorbed East Germany, only to discover that redressing environmental damages in this old Soviet satellite would prove to be a huge drag on the reunited nation's collective economic development.

It is not hard to envision circumstances under which nasty environment "surprises" force even more drastic upward revisions of estimated spending on green goods around the globe. These surprises might involve larger holes in the ozone layer, global warming, massive flooding linked to deforestation in Asia, another Chernobyl disaster involving a nuclear reactor in Eastern Europe, a series of Bhopal-caliber tragedies resulting from air inversions combined with excessive auto emissions.

One need not be of an especially apocalyptic bent to see what *might* happen in the aftermath of such happenings when it comes to a perceived need for sharp increases in environmental spending. Environmental problems are so varied and endemic, spending growth in this field has become a near-statistical certainty.

Whether prudent government and business planning or spasmodic crisis management and damage control precipitates heightened environmental spending, many U.S. green companies are well positioned to benefit. Though we have lost our lead in several environmental technical specialties in which we were once totally dominant, we remain more than competitive when it comes to technologies such as emissions reduction, recycling, and waste processing.

Just as American companies move to tap international green markets, however, foreign companies move to get pieces of our own domestic green business. In the solid and hazardous waste-handling fields, Canadian-based Laidlaw, Inc., British-controlled Atwoods plc., and Australian-owned Brambles have emerged as major players on these shores. In the air pollution control sector, the Swedish-Swiss engineering giant Asea Brown Boveri has captured a very large percentage of the American market and begun to penetrate other business areas as well (though America's Ogden Corporation agreed to buy Boveri's waste-to-energy business in 1992).

Other foreign entities are seeking their own shares of the American environmental cleanup business. British Nuclear Fuels and France's Cogema are vying for larger roles in this country's nuclear cleanup. Denmark's Novo Nordisk has emerged as a strong participant in our biopesticide market.

Japanese industrial giants Fuji Electric and Nippon Steel, which are very seriously pursuing environmental infrastructure project opportunities around the world, are increasingly active on American shores in the environmental cleanup market through joint ventures and subsidiaries. Japanese environmental product specialist Kurita Water Industries, meanwhile, is working hard to win greater market share here as well.

This vast internationalization of the U.S. and worldwide environmental cleanup markets, this proliferation of domestic and foreign firms active in the green trades, is both a natural and a positive overall development. What is less favorable from the American perspective is the nagging suspicion that our government's attitude toward "the environment" as a problem rather than an opportunity during the 1980s and early 1990s may have undermined our capacity to compete in the green trades in years to come.

As recently as the United Nations–sponsored conference on the environment held in Rio de Janeiro in June 1992, the U.S. government was so little interested in fostering export of American green goods, it failed to support vigorously our national participation in the huge trade event that was part of the conference. While only 25 U.S. companies made an appearance at this event, Japan fielded 130 companies, and even mainland China had more than 70 in attendance.

Will the United States again fail to end up with the economic goodies in a field it largely created and once dominated? Are we destined now, at the end of the twentieth century, to play the role toward Japan and Germany that England played toward us at the start of this century—the role of a brilliant technical pioneer without the practical smarts to benefit from its own innovations?

Karmically speaking, it would be perfectly appropriate if this were to happen when it comes to the green trades and their associated jobs and profits. Some Americans, however, would prefer not to accept such a destiny.

The record of a new Clinton administration in this sphere is yet to be written.

SEVEN

ON THE ENTREPRENEURIAL FRONT

An economy, like a pyramid, is mostly constructed of large building blocks, piled one atop the other. We have described how the large sector-blocks comprising the U.S. economy are today undergoing an environmental reshaping and how the entire edifice has been enlarged in recent years through addition of a new building block, the environmental cleanup industry.

Like a pyramid, however, no economy is fully finished without some kind of mortar joining together its various parts and filling in its countless cracks. This is the role played by small-business entrepreneurs in the American economic system. In a fast-greening economy, it is a role increasingly played by enomic entrepreneurs.

Certainly, not all environmental businesses today are small. Waste Management and its subsidiaries, this country's largest private environmental cleanup entity, had revenues during 1992 in excess of $8.6 billion.

Some vendors associated with "natural" products also have become very substantial enterprises. The Body Shop grew from a single store in 1976 to a 700-store worldwide operation with $544 million in retail sales by the end of 1991.

When it comes to enomic businesses generally, however, an overwhelming majority of the estimated 65,000 to 70,000 American firms involved in some kind of environmental cleanup, and the thousands more that are otherwise "green" by virtue of making, selling, installing, or creating environment-saving products or concepts, are smallish ventures with few employees or run by a single proprietor.

These enomic entrepreneurs exude the same vitality so much in evidence wherever people freely and with knowledge aforethought enter into the underfunded, understaffed, and invariably overburdened voluntary servitude that characterizes the working lives of almost all American small businesspeople. The keen identification these individuals usually feel for their role in helping bring about transcendentally important ecological ends merely enhances their kenetic levels.

As new enomic realities sweep through the American marketplace, environmentalist "movement" people are becoming less and less relevant when it comes to shaping economic policies directly (though their efforts continue to be quite relevant indirectly, through raising environmental consciousness in ways that change consumers' buying preferences). Enomic entrepreneurs, meanwhile, are becoming ever more important as vectors linking 1960s-like environmental idealism to jobs and profits in the 1990s.

Just as there is a life-cycle pattern to environmental employment among people who work for other people (described in Chapter 5), a similar pattern is discernible when it comes to green entrepreneurship. Enomic enterprise in the 1990s is a very different animal from what it was a couple of decades back at the time of the first Earth Day.

Then, it largely consisted of novelty peddling (T-shirts, posters, bumper stickers, and so on), political and legal advocacy, and first-generation recycling activities that for all practical purposes were traditional junkyard operations fronted by an earth logo. Today green enterprise has evolved into an extraordinarily diverse and pervasive set of activities serving an economy undergoing an overall environment-related overhaul.

There is no comprehensive way in which to address the current green entrepreneurship phenomenon adequately. It encompasses too many separate parts and pieces that do not lend themselves to easy categorization.

Indeed, one would be hard-pressed to find an American with independent business propensities who has not sat down with friends of similar suasion in recent years and come up with at least half a dozen plausible ideas that would fit under the umbrella of enomic entrepreneurship. Just as once upon a time every would-be innovator in this country wanted to do something with cars, and later with computers, today he or she is thinking green.

Entire books, such as Steven Bennett's 1991 *Ecopreneuring*, have looked at this burgeoning field. *IN BUSINESS* magazine, which bills itself "The Magazine for Environmental Entrepreneuring," was obliged to use twenty-three distinct classifications in its 1992 update of environmental entrepreneurs to try to encompass the field—and still was far from covering all its elements.

Perhaps the only way even to suggest what enomic enterprise means to the contemporary American economy, and what it might mean in years to come, is to focus on a few areas where present green business activity is most intense. The following examples consist of recycling enterprises, food raising and selling, gardening, media and communications, the professions, retailing, alternative energy generation, and conservation.

These examples are largely culled from business publications such as the *Wall Street Journal*, dailies including the *New York Times* and *Philadelphia Inquirer*, and trade magazines such as *IN BUSINESS* and *Biocycle*. Readers, of course, are invited to adorn these examples with their own stock of comeupons in order to get a better sense that, yes, this *is*, most certainly, where it is at nowadays, for those seeking the exquisite pleasures and perils of self-employment.

Retailing is among the most popular ecoentrepreneurial activities. Though major mass-merchandising chains are handling more and more earth-friendly products, the public still tends to associate such goods with "alternative" stores, which are still usually smallish operations.

Retailing attracts many enomic entrepreneurs because it is a business with low capital entry requirements. It is also a business where success often can be attained without huge promotional expenditures, using word-of-mouth to attract customers. Though an increasing number of ecoretailers are opening for business today, and even finding their way into malls, overstoring, too, is still not a major problem in most markets.

Other generic attractions of ecoretailing include possibilities for higher markups on goods because the number of competing stores selling similar goods is not yet great, and generally fewer problems with theft because these outlets tend to attract less theft-prone shoppers. Would-be thieves, after all, are more likely to go to a K-mart and grab some sweaters and personal appliances than go for a bag of mulch or a yogurt maker at a local green outlet.

Though ecoretailing is nationwide, it is stronger in some parts of the country than others. Not surprisingly, California leads the way here. Companies such as Natural Wonders, which had eighty-eight stores in operation by the start of 1993, is headquartered in the state. Eco-malls, like one operating in Santa Monica, are beginning to appear there as well.

As noted in the last chapter, recycling and related environmentally sound reuse techniques have evolved into mainstream businesses. All major collectors, buriers, and incinerators of hazardous and nonhazardous waste practice some variety of the craft. Thousands of cities and towns employ curbside collection, and hundreds have composting programs in place or on the drawing boards for their wastewater sludges.

Tens of thousands of private companies recycle their own office and cafeteria wastes or practice resource recovery in their manufacturing facilities. Utilities around the nation are recycling waste heat through cogeneration.

This vast "big boy" recycling network, however, has in no way displaced entrepreneurial recyclers. It merely complements their efforts. Opportunities for small operators in this field continue to proliferate. They remain so prevalent, in fact, that entrepreneurial recycling merits as much attention as the large corporate and governmental programs previously cited.

Where are the growing edges of entrepreneurial recycling today? As bigger entities co-opt increasing shares of traditional paper, cardboard, glass, and metals markets, smaller recycling firms move more and more into niche specialties.

Companies like Corporate Conservation in Massachusetts successfully recycle office papers (including computer varieties) as well as other office-generated throw-aways. Other specialists provide comparable services involving wrapping and packaging wastes for retailers eager to please more environmentally aware clienteles.

Still other consultant recyclers are structuring programs for hotels, motels, and casinos from Vegas to Atlantic City. A growing number of these hoteliers, it might be added, are offering their own guests "green rooms" for premium prices. Such rooms are not only free of old tobacco fumes, they feature organic soap in the shower and bottled water in the fridge.

Bell Atlantic and other giant public companies are greening their annual reports by using more recycled papers and less environmentally damaging inks. Other giants, including Chevron, Du Pont, and Rohm and Haas, are even putting out separate "green annual reports" to complement the usual yearly statements they send to stockholders. Entrepreneurs are doing comparable green annual report make-overs for hundreds of smaller public companies that need to project positive images to the investment community.

Each new environmental regulation—scads of which are appearing all the time—seems to kick off new opportunities for niche market recycling. A recent EPA ruling aimed at reducing the amount of mercury escaping from old fluorescent lamps into the groundwater under landfills, by way of example, gave a business boost to companies with names like Lighting Recycling in Massachusetts and Technical Salvage and Environmental Engineering in Minnesota.

Some 242 million car and truck tires are discarded each year in the United States, joining the 2 or 3 billion already soaking up rain in lots and fields around the country. They are an incredible burden to municipal officials who are charged with disposing of most of them (some four million are dumped in New York City alone each year) and an equally incredible source of new opportunities for reusers and recyclers large and small.

Some big boys such as Texaco are beginning to burn millions of these tires safely to generate electricity. Other millions are now being mixed with asphalt to create a road surfacing material, in order to comply with provisions of the 1991 Federal Highway Act. Many more formerly discarded tires are being retreaded and turned back into usable tires, a trend that will grow faster after tire makers solve all the technical problems related to recycling (or plucking out) the steel bands used to reinforce newer tires.

Millions of other tires, however, are now collected by entrepreneurs and used to build jetties and reefs, to construct entire houses, or converted into floor tiles. A company called DejaShoe in Oregon even combines a number of discarded materials (including tires) to manufacture new footwear.

Innumerable small companies today (as well as giants like Exxon) collect and recycle used auto fluids. The most popular is waste lube oil, which is processed and turned back into lubricants, instead of being burned in industrial boilers as was the usual fate of this material for many years.

Machines that let garage owners turn used lube back into reusable lube are now becoming available, though they are still too costly for many small service station operators. These same operators, it might be noted, are seeing their facilities gradually evolve into emissions checking and reduction centers, as an overall economic greening reshapes the repair and maintenance sectors of the U.S. economy.

"Plastics," whispered a family friend offering avuncular advice to a confused Dustin Hoffman in the 1967 film *The Graduate*. He was referring to the economic potential of manufacturing with virgin plastics in the 1960s.

In the 1990s, the potential for making things out of used stocks of plastic looks almost as good. While leading soft drink sellers and packagers are recycling old beverage containers into new ones and other "biggies" are successfully incorporating old PET plastic into fiberfill that ends up in carpeting, entrepreneurs are turning the stuff into everything from new park benches, to toys, to building insulation, to party confetti.

In the rag trades, stores selling used clothing continue to be popular not only with the down-and-out and the old-line thrifty, but with a younger generation of shoppers who view used clothes as a kind of recycling fashion and political statement. Collecting and turning in used aluminum cans for the deposits they bring in many cities is now the largest source of legal income for many street people.

A company in Philadelphia reuses mislabeled food products, which once would have ended up as organic trash sent to landfills, by turning them into animal feed. The Farm Share program in Florida, meanwhile, recycles perfectly edible vegetables that used to be dumped on fields as fertilizer, because they did not meet visually pleasing standards expected by supermarket shoppers, into giveaways for poor Americans.

Slowly but surely, people are coming to recognize in this country's waste streams a national mother lode for scores of resources. The modern small-scale recycler can thus be compared to the lone prospectors of the last century who skirted the claims of big mining operations (with their huge investments in modern equipment and hefty payrolls) in search of more widely dispersed and exotic sources of wealth hidden deeper in the hinterlands.

All up and down the food chain (as that term applies to the American diet), new environment-linked considerations are asserting themselves. Having largely accepted the dictum that "you are what you eat," Americans have begun looking closely at how food is grown on conventional farms, and not infrequently become quite alarmed about how agricultural chemicals might be affecting their health.

They have also become concerned about other food sources, such as fish, and about contamination threats to trees and other nonedible plants. All these worries have opened up enormous new opportunities for enomic entrepreneurship as it applies to what is grown, how it is grown, and where it is sold after it is grown.

One interesting manifestation of the growing emphasis on what is grown are new plants being raised for their natural plastic content. Plastics from plants, instead of plastics from petrochemicals, could soon mean easier natural biodegradation that goes a long way toward solving many disposal problems currently faced by the packaging industry.

Collecting indigenous plants that are used to rehabilitate land after it has been extensively mined or otherwise "developed" has brought into being eco-firms like Utah-based Mapleleaf Seed Company and Granite Seed. Inoculating plants with mycorrhizal fungus to make their root systems better able to cope with badly polluted soil is generating revenues for enomic entrepreneurial companies, including Pennsylvania's Mycorr Tech.

Among Americans, interest in cultivating nature has surged. According to the National Gardening Association, retail sales of flower, vegetable, berry, and herb items at lawn and garden outlets jumped from $15.5 billion in 1988 to $22.1 billion in 1991. Some idea of how organic marketing is becoming even more organic these days, was to be found in a 1991 book entitled *The Green Consumer*, which had a whole section on what were termed "Low-Impact Garden Supply Companies."

The Ringer Corporation in Minnesota now generates more than $20 million a year in sales serving the needs of such ultra–green-minded lawn and garden product buyers. Some of these shoppers are also purchasing mulching aids produced by smaller firms, including Environmental Applied Products in Idaho and DJK Enterprises in Iowa. Gardeners looking for really fashionable, upscale fertilizers can now buy premium rhino or elephant manure from several zoos around the country.

For people who prefer to kill weeds with scalding water rather than herbicides, a Minnesota company called Aqua Heat Technologies has a device to do the job. For people who decide that what is really lacking in their gardens is more worms, a company in North Carolina will fill the need with its Worm-A-Way line.

Organic wines made from grapes grown without chemicals are being produced by some of this country's largest vintners. But they are still a specialty of scores of smaller wineries as well. Today, also, one can buy countless organic food products through the mail, including items like Hillbilly Bean Soap.

Pond aquaculture has long been popular in parts of Asia because it provides much-needed protein for poor inland farmers. In recent years it has become a burgeoning, largely ma-and-pa economic activity in this country, because so many fresh and ocean waters are perceived to be so seriously contaminated by pollution that people are deeply concerned about mercury and other toxics in their fillets. If one looks to the waters for packaging materials as well as sustenance, biodegradable foams made from seaweed are also coming to market from entrepreneurs.

Just as organic (and perhaps designer) seafood from small producers is gaining popularity among more and more Americans, so, too, is organic beef. This food comes from cattle raised on natural grasses rather than pesticided grains.

At the retail end of the greening American food chain are an estimated 6,000 mostly small organic food stores. About 150 of these are big enough to qualify as natural food supermarkets. There are even organic food chains, the three largest of which in 1990, according to *IN BUSINESS* Magazine (Mrs. Gooch's, Whole Food Markets, and Bread & Circus) grossed more than $210 million. To accommodate the changing food views of American society's most traditional junk food addicts, high schoolers, a newsletter for teenage vegetarians called *How On Earth* (HOE) is now being published.

Literally thousands of restaurants around the country have a green tinge on their current menus. A growing number are fully greened, like Macheezmo Mouse in Oregon, which specializes in Mexican-style food. Some restaurant operators use plants on their premises to help clean the air. Some use natural grease-eating bacteria supplied by Florida's Environmental Biotech, Inc., to help clean their kitchens.

Beyond the impressive number and collective dollar volume represented by these increasingly enomic food and fiber enterprises is the sheer dynamism they bring to their respective sectors of the economy. In a very real sense, this is where much of the food and fiber industries' greatest vitality and innovation is now to be found.

Just as recycling has gone from an "alternative" approach to waste management in the 1960s, to a part of virtually all mainstream waste management programs in the present decade, conservation and nontraditional ways to generate energy have likewise gone mainstream, as the United States seeks a better balance between its own 5 percent share of the world's population and its consumption of 25 percent of the world's energy. Ecoentrepreneurs, of course, continue to lead the way in this new balancing act.

The Rocky Mountain Institute in Colorado estimates that investment in energy conservation in this country now exceeds $5 billion annually. Large numbers of energy consulting firms have sprung up to take advantage of this growth market.

Xenergy in Massachusetts, for example, helps utilities establish conservation programs—and earned some $20 million doing so in 1991. Smaller firms, such as Rising Sun Enterprises and Proven Alternatives, help other businesses save on their lighting and other power costs, or help architects plan more energy-efficient structures.

Because of a personal commitment to "deep ecology," or a heightened sense of thrift, or maybe just out of plain curmudgeonliness, many Americans are deciding to seek freedom from utility grids. This has opened up opportunities for makers of wind power generators, such as Vermont-based NGV Systems, and mail-order sellers of solar and other off-grid energy products, such as California's Real Goods Trading Corporation. It also has meant business for purveyors of water- and energy-saving showerheads, along with products like composting toilets.

In today's very difficult business climate, enomic enterprise keyed to energy saving and alternative means of power generation is not a sure—or even an easy—road to riches. Perhaps, as some experts predict, windpower generating equipment (much of it manufactured by small firms) will be meeting 10 to 15 percent of this country's total power needs by the year 2020. But in a nearer time frame, the world's largest solar electric company, Lutz International, filed for bankruptcy in 1991, and many smaller solar thermal and electric companies have met similar fates.

From the enomic perspective, however, the success rate for entrepreneurial energy conservation and energy producing operations is less important than the rate at which they are entering the marketplace. Enomics animates an economy, but no free market factor rewards everyone.

The recently depressed state of free market housing in this country has likewise worked against the interests of many enomic entrepreneurs who sell their wares and services to homeowners. This will likely continue until demand for new homes improves, especially in eco-conscious California, and stimulates buying of more products like highly insulated windows which help protect the environment by saving energy, along with advanced composting systems for kitchens as well as the garden.

Entrepreneurial professionals in many fields are now deriving maximum economic benefits from "the environment." Their numbers are not great compared to enomic recycling, consulting, or retailing entrepreneurs. But their proliferation in recent years illustrates how a pervasive economic greening is reshaping professions as well as trades, the arts, the sciences, and general business service sectors.

The archetypal enomic profession, of course, is the law. An estimated 22,000 American lawyers now practice under the banner of environmental specialist. In addition, through activities involving property transfers and other highly environment-sensitive legal doings, a far greater number are occasional practitioners of environmental law.

What makes these activities "entrepreneurial" rather than just meeting market needs is the ability of lawyers to create or complexify the law in ways that vastly magnify their own economic interests. The classic example of how this approach operates is to be found in the legal entrepreneuring that has gone into this country's Superfund site cleanup.

Though the federal Superfund law was passed in 1980, between 1980 and 1992 only eighty-four sites that have appeared on the EPA's priority cleanup list over the years were fully rehabilitated and restored. In this same period, according to at least one study, approximately 90 percent of all Superfund spending went toward various transactional costs (such as legal fees) rather than actual cleanup, while 90 percent of all sums released by insurers to settle Superfund claims ended up as legal fees and litigation-related costs.

Tens of thousands of cases involving asbestos contamination damages to health and property have likewise wended their way through the court system since the early 1980s. Lawyers have garnered most of the settlements in these disputes as well.

Looking down the road, equally green pastures of plenty for attorneys will almost certainly accrue from lead poisoning litigation. After the Center for Disease Control in late 1992 raised its estimate of the number of schoolchildren in Philadelphia exposed to lead dangers from 22,000 to more than 90,000, a seminar on lead paint dangers in that city attracted more than 300 lawyers.

Workplace-related environmental litigation opportunities are still another mushrooming source of lawyer revenues. An official at the National Institute of Occupational Safety and Health in Denver has estimated that as much as 1 percent of the entire U.S. workforce (about a million people) regularly take home toxic materials from their factories, mines, and offices. It is virtually certain this will generate much litigation in years to come.

All this highly profitable green lawyering is neither "good" nor "bad" from the enomic standpoint. It simply is. It is just another manifestation of how a greening economy means more opportunities for one part of the American entrepreneurial work force.

Other professionals now creating lucrative enomic niches

for themselves include Wall Streeters who raise venture capital for environmental businesses and people who run environmental mutual funds. By the start of this decade, there were five mutual funds investing in companies that actually clean the environment (Fidelity Select Environmental Services, Freedom Environmental Fund, Kemper Environmental Services Fund, Oppenheimer Global Environmental Fund, and the Schield Progressive Environmental Fund).

Several times this number invest their capital using "socially responsible" screening criteria that include how a company's operations pollute the environment. The Calvert Social Investment family of funds is the largest entity in this latter category.

During the protracted Uruguay Round of international trade negotiations, which ran from the late 1980s through the early 1990s, so-called intellectual rights were a major topic of discussion. The reason disagreements here were so intense for so long was because so much money is at stake when it comes to who creates materials that end up in everything from books, to song lyrics, to movies, to pieces of computer software.

And what is the enomic stake in all this? Artists and intellectuals are the purest of entrepreneurs. They also tend to be one of the groups in society most concerned about the natural environment. This concern is reflected in artistic and intellectual properties that are not only sold domestically but exported around the world.

Books about "the environment" are today a major pillar of the book publishing industry. As the bibliography of this volume suggests, even works more tightly focused on the environment and business, or the environment and economics, now make up a fast-growing publishing niche.

Nonbook publishing ventures covering some aspect of the environment are even more in evidence. They include nature magazines, publications that focus on some specialized area of compliance, business periodicals with names like *ECO* and *IN BUSINESS*. There are also a score of more generalized publications, including *GARBAGE*, along with many hundred newsletters. Every week brings a new set of entries into the computer software program environmental compliance market.

Beyond the print and software media, sculptors, painters, and conceptual artists including Richard Kamler, Kay Wood and Mel Chin, along with a growing numbers of concert hall composers and performers, are finding inspiration for the work in the fight to save the planet. The same is true for architects like Michael Reynolds and for a growing group of fashion and interior designers, including Hilton McConnico.

Meanwhile, in a more pop vein, Bo Diddly has recorded a song with a green message. Ecothemes form the basis of entire low-brow films, such as *The Toxic Avenger*, make cameo appearances in Robo-Cop films, and even turn up in the form of an ecologically correct kitchen in Martin Scorsese's *Cape Fear*. Combating evil polluters is a staple in countless prime-time macho police dramas and children's cartoons.

The arts are going green. So, too, is the arts industry and its many affiliates, including communication media such as public relations and advertising. So, therefore, by definition, is artistic entrepreneurship.

When it comes to the reality of enomic entrepreneurship in the United States today, the kinds of opportunities opening up and their potential is limited only by one's imagination. Various statistics and examples detail the truth of this view. But it is much more a subjective than a statistical truth, because it involves countless business activities crisscrossing the entire economic spectrum, about which hard statistics can never become available.

Personal anecdotal evidence here is as close to economic truth as one is likely to get in this realm. For a growing number of economy watchers, however, such evidence is becoming overwhelming.

EIGHT

THE NEW AMERICAN ENVIRONMENTAL GEOGRAPHY

"All politics is local" is a well-known axiom among campaigners for public office. "Think globally, act locally" is an environmentalist equivalent. For people taking an enomic view of the American economy, a comparable axiom might be phrased: "All aspects of the new environmental economics have a distinctive local flavor."

In past chapters, we looked at ways in which different sectors of the U.S. economy (transportation, petrochemicals, utilities, agriculture, etc.) and different functions of this economy (manufacturing, marketing, and the like) are undergoing enomic transformations. Here we examine ways in which different areas of the country are undergoing their own enomic transformations.

Until recently, a discussion of "the environmental geography of the United States" would have revolved around pockets of pollution in different states and regions. About air problems in different cities. About the water quality of various inland waterways. About soil contamination due to chemical pesticide run-offs in the farm belt and acid rain deposits in the upper Midwest and New York State.

Such a discussion, in other words, would have been conducted within a purely *ecological* framework. Today the economic component of this geographic equation also would enter
strongly into the conversation.

It would be hard to exaggerate the current and future
importance of environmental factors as they affect economic
development within various American cities, states, and regions. Such is the underlying basis of the New American Environmental Geography.

This new environmental geography explains why businesspeople making economic plans have learned to focus very
closely on present and projected environmental overhead in
places where they hope to do business—costs to which they
might be obliged to contribute through local taxation. It explains the newfound interest of these same businesspeople in
local environmental infrastructure as it affects air and water
quality, on local access to quality environmental services, and
perhaps on local environmental marketing opportunities as
well.

This is also why local government planners have become
so tuned into the concept of a new American environmental
geography. The subject is increasingly important when planners apply it to their own budget allocations. Put simply: If
more public money must be spent getting asbestos out of
schools, monitoring urban air quality, and the like, less will be
available for police protection and repairing potholes.

In November 1992, by way of illustration, 150 separate
government agencies in southern California agreed to pay a
total of more than $45 million over four years as their contribu-
tion to clean up a chemical release that tainted four counties.
(A number of chemical firms agreed to come up with even
more as part of this same settlement.) Will this $45 million be
translated into reduced services or higher taxes to support some
of these government agencies? Almost certainly.

The upside of this localized green bookkeeping includes
the growth of environmental cleanup firms that earn billions
of dollars and create thousands of new jobs in areas where
they settle and expand. One shorthand way to appreciate this

positive enomic consequence is to focus on where the cleanup industry is experiencing its most pronounced growth.

With so many thousand U.S. firms specializing in some form of monitoring, testing, and remediation work, outposts of this industry are of course everywhere. But a look at where just the seventy largest publicly traded waste-handling "majors" are headquartered—companies with collective revenues in 1992 of more than $31 billion and domestic payrolls in excess of 130,000 employees—reveals some interesting geographic patterns.

A striking eight of these seventy firms are headquartered in a single city, Houston. They are Allwaste, Browning-Ferris, Critical Industries, the GNI Group, Gundle Environmental Systems, Republic Waste Industries, Sanifill, and the Vallen Corporation. The obvious explanation for this concentration is that Houston is the hub of one of this country's most important petroleum-producing and chemical-making regions. Petroleum and chemicals cause pollution. Local firms emerge to clean it up.

Approximately 50,000 exploration, production, refining, and related jobs were lost nationally in both 1990 and 1991, a goodly number of them in the Houston area. The economic base of that city, which was 83 percent dependent on such functions in 1981, was only 60 percent dependent a decade later. The cleanup end of the petro-chemical business was part of the economic diversification that helped Houston's job picture stay relatively strong after local exploration and production opportunities slumped.

A similar process of cleanup job creation occurred in the chemical-making belt in the Delaware Valley, which includes much of New Jersey, down through eastern Pennsylvania, and into the state of Delaware. A former EPA Regional Administrator has dubbed this region "the Silicon Valley of the environmental services industry" because of its heavy concentration of cleanup firms.

Eleven of this country's largest publicly traded cleanup companies are based in the Delaware Valley: Air & Water Technologies, Betz Laboratories, Envirosafe Services, Environmental Control Group, Handex Environmental Recovery, Horsehead Resource Development, Met-Pro Corporation, Ogden Projects, Rollins Environmental, Wellman, and Roy F. Weston, Inc.

The old Rust Belt region of the industrial Northeast, running from Buffalo, New York, through western Pennsylvania, Ohio, and west to Indiana and Illinois, was notorious for its pollution in the 1950s and 1960s. Not surprisingly, this area too now headquarters a hefty share of the environmental services' "top-seventy." They include American Waste Services, Calgon Carbon, Canonie Environmental Services, Chambers Development, Chemical Waste Management, CPAC, Ecology & Environment, Geraghty & Miller, Integrated Waste Systems, Landauer, Inc., Mid-American Waste Systems, Nalco Chemical, OHM Corporation, Resource Recycling Technologies, Safety-Kleen, Sevenson Environmental, Waste Management, Inc. and Zurn Industries.

California, with its many industrial facilities and exceptionally strong environmental laws, boasts another concentration of environmental cleanup majors. Six of the top-seventy firms are headquartered in the state: American Ecology Corporation, Earth Technology Corporation (USA), EMCON Associates, Harding Associates, International Technology Corporation, and Western Waste Industries.

Economists and government planners have long tended to view cleaning up past pollution and preventing future pollution as a necessary but nonetheless unfortunate millstone borne by the entire U.S. economy. As the above suggests, however, the cleanup process also can be an engine of economic growth—especially in areas like the Rust Belt and the Oil Patch, which went into economic tailspins when their traditional industries faltered.

As noted throughout this book, the environmental cleanup industry per se is very far from being the only measure of a greening U.S. economic system. Where leaders of this industry are headquartered is therefore only a quickie gauge of the total effects of the environment on local economies.

The need to portray a new environmental economics with a broader brush, showing the economic upsides and downsides of regional enomics, is thus apparent. Again though, as is the case with the corporate, industry, and national enomic profiles offered earlier, readers must keep in mind that the following examples are suggestive, not comprehensive. Almost certainly, in years to come, each of the profiles compressed here into a few paragraphs will be the subject of voluminous studies.

A look at Pennsylvania hints at the ways in which one of this country's biggest industrial states is being buffeted by waste-handling problems while also enjoying many benefits of waste-related enomic growth.

If Pennsylvania was a sovereign nation, waste would be a mainstay of its national economy. The Keystone State is one of this country's largest processors of trash, not only its own considerable output, but some 3.2 million tons shipped in annually from elsewhere, especially New York and New Jersey.

Beginning in the early 1990s, a long-projected national "shortage" of solid-waste landfills and incinerating facilities evaporated. Excess trash-handling capacities came into being. Prices paid landfill operators leveled off and, in many places, even began to fall sharply.

This had a negative impact on the Pennsylvania trash industry, but a positive impact on the city budgets of major trash-producing urban centers such as Philadelphia. Both impacts reflect new enomic geographic realities.

Thirteen states allow toxic chemical wastes to be incinerated within their borders. Additional states permit these wastes to be buried in specially designed facilities. Pennsylvania does not have its own permanent incineration or burial disposal facility for hazardous wastes (though one is currently in the long and torturous process of being approved and constructed).

According to a state publication, some thirty-five industries doing business in Pennsylvania generate substantial amounts of hazardous wastes as part of their regular operations. The biggest generators are steel works, chemical plants, and electric machinery producers.

Until a local hazardous waste facility is in operation,

therefore, all these businesses are obliged to send money out of state to cover costs of this nasty but necessary disposal. It should be added, however, that costs of toxic waste disposal for the Keystone State's chemical industry have fallen in recent years because better in-plant controls reduced the amount of toxic materials generated by the industry 12 percent between 1987 and 1990. A recession and installation of much more efficient equipment have worked to moderate toxic waste produced by the local steel industry as well.

Thousands of Pennsylvania health care facilities ship "red bag" wastes by the truckload to Kentucky, Tennessee, and Mississippi, which have become centers for final handling of these dangerous throw-aways. Additional tons of low-level nuclear waste are shipped to South Carolina, Nevada, and Washington State for permanent burial.

Under provisions of a regional agreement known as the Appalachian Low-Level Waste Compact, Pennsylvania by 1996 is slated to be home to one of the ten facilities that will not only handle the state's own low-level nuclear wastes, but will receive imports of the stuff from neighboring states West Virginia, Maryland, and Delaware. This is only fair, since Pennsylvania is in fact the nation's biggest producer of such low-level nuclear wastes, largely by virtue of its nine resident nuclear power plants. Some 81 percent of the state's nuclear waste is power-plant generated.

To cite just a few other environment-linked factors dramatically affecting Pennsylvania's overall economy today, the state's forestry industry (one of the largest in the country) is among the most damaged by acid rain. Its coal mining industry has enormous liabilities related to redressing past damages to forests and waterways as mandated by various federal and local statutes.

The state's largest city, Philadelphia, has some of the dirtiest urban air in the country. Philly motorists will therefore be obliged to pay higher gasoline prices to burn cleaner fuels in years to come, cutting into their disposable incomes.

Under terms of the 1990 federal Clean Air Act, which seeks to reduce automobile commuting by 25 percent, employers in Philadelphia and other heavily smogged cities will have to find ways to encourage their employees to carpool. Possible economic spinoffs of this new enomic reality might include fewer local car sales.

Still another facet of the Philadelphia story as seen from the perspective of a new enomic geography involves water bills. A 1992 EPA study found that 130 of this country's largest water systems (including Philadelphia's) exceeded that agency's permitted lead levels. Not coincidentally, to address this and other clean water requirements, Philadelphia's water department in 1992 asked for a 28 percent rate increase.

Such an increase can be viewed as an enomic wealth transfer from Philly residents to city government. And of course, enomic transfers like this are becoming a commonplace in other parts of the country as well. In Boston, which has the country's highest water rates because 90 percent of the Boston Harbor cleanup is being paid for locally instead of by the state or federal governments, average household water and sewer bills are expected to average almost $1,200 by 1996 and $1,600 by the end of this decade.

The intensity of Pennsylvania's waste needs and its indigenous waste-handling capabilities have worked to make it a natural center for local growth of environmental services and pollution control firms. Eight of the country's seventy largest publicly traded waste-handling entities are headquartered there. Together, by the end of 1990, these eight companies employed more than 13,000 people and generated annual revenues in excess of $2 billion.

Along with "exporting" green goods to other parts of the United States, Pennsylvania-based environmental firms are increasingly contributing to U.S. environmental exports abroad. In 1989, for example, Calgon Carbon earned $87.3 million from sales in Europe, up from $72.9 million the year before. Also in 1989, Met-Pro sold $524,086 worth of pollution control systems abroad, up from $294,616 the year before.

By 1991 Pennsylvania was the state with the seventh largest overall exports to Mexico. Not surprisingly, a fair share of these exports consisted of various kinds of green goods.

Along with environmental company headquarters, there are scores of "outpost" offices of other environmental majors in Pennsylvania. Hundreds of private (non–publicly held) environmental companies also are headquartered in the state. Some, such as the ERM Group, are fairly significant in terms of size.

Large educational institutions such as the University of Pennsylvania in Philadelphia have their own environmental education programs, which boost the local economy by attracting out-of-state students. The university's Center for Energy and the Environment is an outgrowth of the National Center for Energy Management and Power, founded in 1971, with a current curriculum reflecting 1990s' environmental concerns.

The costs of cleaning up past pollution and preventing future varieties has been said to contribute to the loss of old-line heavy industry in long-industrialized Pennsylvania. Pittsburgh, and its traditional steel and coal industries, is frequently cited as an example of this environment-costs-jobs-and-profits paradigm.

The city of Pittsburgh today, however, is enjoying a splendid postsmokestack renaissance. It is as prosperous (in a downscaled sort of way) as ever and far, far less polluted in the bargain. The city Charles Dickens once called "hell with the lid lifted" is, in fact, an exemplar of enomic development.

One of nature's own best environmental cleaning agents is largely responsible for bringing the city's air quality back to normal so quickly. Pittsburgh is blessed with more trees per acre than any other American city—though very active tree-planting campaigns initiated in such places as Chicago and San Francisco may soon challenge this premier position.

The mills that remain active in Pittsburgh have been retooled into world-class competitive modernity. Local economic diversification into nonmanufacturing, less-polluting pursuits has also proven very helpful in making the city's economy far more recession-resistant than in years past. It is in the field of twenty-first-century railroading, however, where technology and local civic planning seem to be coming together most clearly to create a new enomic synthesis.

The old Steel City's business, labor, and government communities are today well along the way to creating what may be the nation's first operational magnetic levitation (maglev) rail system, a prototypical environmental technology that will initially link the Pittsburgh Airport to the center city, from there spread to other parts of Pennsylvania, West Virginia, and Maryland, and possibly expand at some later date to points farther west and east.

Maglevs may one day make Pittsburgh the Detroit of enomic mass transit. At the least, this green technology will create a very strong demand for locally produced engineered metal alloys, locally generated electric power, and locally available skilled labor.

The creation by the University of Pittsburgh Trust and the EPA in 1988 of a National Environmental Technology Applications Corporation (NETAC), designed to help commercialize leading edge environmental products and techniques, also bodes well for helping Pittsburgh become a key node in America's environmental techno-infrastructure. Other large American cities now moving in this same direction include Seattle and Minneapolis, places where the right mix of educational institutions, a farsighted business community and a progressive city government, are in place with a vision.

As even this brief survey demonstrates, an extraordinary number of economic variables must be considered in the new enomic geography of the Keystone State. Beyond the obvious and relatively significant ones noted, countless "little things" with the potential to run up unwanted environmental costs or boost desired green business activity exist.

These include positive factors, such as savings realized by municipal taxpayers when autumn leaves are mulched rather than disposed of in landfills, and negative factors, such as a current near-total failure to recycle dangerous toxic household chemicals (cleaning solvents, and the like), which ultimately affect health care costs in Pennsylvania. Little things.

Clearly, the overall economy of the Keystone State is now as waste based, for better or worse, as it is manufacturing or service based. Any economic analysis that does not recognize this fact today is deeply flawed.

Without going into the same detail employed with our Pennsylvania case study, it is worth jumping around the United States a bit to see how enomics and locality now play out together. This junket is not systematic. A shotgun approach better serves to make the point that a new enomic geography is emerging *everywhere*.

Consider from this perspective Massachusetts. The "Massachusetts Miracle" that got Governor Michael Dukakis nominated for president by the Democratic Party in 1988 dissipated almost immediately after that year's presidential election. It turned out to be based too narrowly on a computer industry facing ferocious worldwide competition, on a defense industry with a fast-fading national mission, and on a real estate boom built on spiraling price expectations almost as fatuous as Holland's seventeenth-century Tulip Mania.

Another economic miracle, however, is today percolating to the surface in the Bay State. The enomic roots of this revitalization promise considerably better staying power.

In 1992 the state's Executive Office of Environmental Affairs and its Environmental Business Council prepared a study that found that Massachusetts' environmental sector garnered some $13 billion in revenues during 1990. A year later another study found that more than 73,000 people were earning an environmental livelihood in the Bay State, working in its 1,300 envirotech companies. According to some estimates, the energy efficiency sector of the envirotech industry (called "demand-side management" when used as a cost-saving tool by utilities) is New England's single fastest-growing business.

Massachusetts, of course, does not exemplify only enomic qualities that bring business, government, and the general public together in perfect harmony. There, as everywhere, a generally benign enomic transition has a way of irritating a great many people. The extremely comprehensive recycling law that got on the state ballot in 1992 (and lost) illustrates this point nicely.

"This proposal," said a spokesman for the Grocery Manufacturers of America, "is the most sweeping, most regressive solid waste proposal we have encountered anywhere, period. Most people think all the crazy ideas come out of California, but even Californians haven't touched this one."

Obviously, not everyone, always, is pleased by the new environmental economic geography. It is as controversial in its near-term effects, as fulsome in its ability to bring economic pain to some people as economic benefit to others, as most other aspects of enomics.

Just as the new enomic geography touches people within the same state in different ways, it also causes conflicts between and among different states. In Massachusetts, for example, one of the country's most successful recycling programs (even before the 1992 measure appeared on the ballot) had succeeded in reducing quantities of garbage destined to end up in the state's eleven trash-to-steam incineration facilities. To keep these incinerators operating full throttle and hence profitably therefore required large trash imports from neighboring Rhode Island.

Because of a deep local recession, however, Rhode Island's Central Landfill was experiencing a shortfall in its own commercial trash collections, where fees had for some time been subsidizing costs of handling the state's municipal trash. To keep down city taxes in Rhode Island, the state moved to restrict garbage exports to Massachusetts.

If these disputes seem to give a new meaning to the term "getting trashed," the situation becomes increasingly cloudy as the geographic dimensions of conflicts about solid waste collection, transportation, and ultimate disposal ripple outward. The same fights over retaining or not retaining trash affecting Rhode Island and Massachusetts also affect government-run and private facilities from Long Island, New York, to cities and towns throughout California.

In Pennsylvania, people in the western part of the state, which accepts large amounts of trash from the eastern part and other states as well, are both glad for the extra revenues that accrue from this activity and angry about being dumped upon. In Indiana, another major trash accepter, political campaigns have been won and lost on opposition to out-of-state garbage. In South Dakota, a huge new landfill that just about everyone in the state seemed to want never opened because falling trash burial fees nationwide made it an uneconomical proposition.

Such regional and interstate hostilities and rivalries get even more intense when they involve more hazardous types of waste. In East Liverpool, Ohio, opening of a hazardous waste treatment facility was blocked for a dozen years by some angry local residents who thought the site chosen for the facility (near a school) was positively crazy; other residents supported the project vigorously because of the jobs and tax revenues it would bring. Then, by the time it came to actually operate the facility in early 1993, some expected sources of toxic waste failed to materialize. Similar disputes and surprises abound at almost all the private and commercial hazardous waste inciner-ators operating anywhere in the country.

The enomic geography involved in most of these conflicts is social as well as sectional. The poorest states, and the poorest parts of the poorest states, have long been the siting grounds (or dumping grounds, if you will) for waste disposal facilities of all kinds.

Cries of "environmental racism" now ring out from the South Bronx, where authorities have occasionally tried to open new solid waste-handling facilities, to Moss Point, Mississippi, a predominantly black community, where other authorities have raised the ire of local residents by siting a medical waste burning installation.

New York City's "Big Apple" economic image is simply the outer skin of a "Big Core" enomic reality involving innu-merable waste problems. For a time in late 1992, for example, it appeared that virtually all new real estate development in the city might be halted because of noncompliance with certain portions of the federal Clean Air Act. Real estate development is one of the major job producers and profit centers in the city.

It is also a prime source of New York's revenues through

property taxes. A recent court ruling concerning a city property assessment that was reduced because the building was tainted with asbestos (and presumably had a lower market value in consequence) raised real worries that urban property taxation generally might have to be lowered because of on-site environmental damages.

A kindred decision about property in New Jersey's Meadowlands, just outside New York City, raised another red flag. There, because federal wetland regulations prevented development, a court also ruled that local property assessments had to be reduced.

Without belaboring the point, property taxes are the basis of municipal solvency. Any threat or even "unsettling" of this tax system, enomic or otherwise, therefore has enormous potential economic implications.

Beyond property values, property maintenance practices within New York, a huge industry employing many thousands of people, is being revolutionized. The *New York Times* has characterized the program as "the most expansive and comprehensive recycling program ever attempted in the United States."

Representing a kind of juncture between urban enomics and urban sociology, this massive recycling effort, even in its early stages, reveals more about life in these United States circa early 1990s than many people might really care to know. Some of the extraordinary difficulties to be faced in making modern American cities greener through recycling were summed up by a Bronx building superintendent who told a *Times* reporter: "Where I live people don't have jobs. They have drug problems. They have crime problems. And the city thinks I'm going to get them to dump their recycling trash in translucent blue bags? I don't even know what a translucent blue bag is."

Then there is the matter of drinking water and wastewater. New York has long been famous for its excellent supplies of the former, piped in from pure upstate sources. Protecting the watershed from which these sources are drawn, however, will require costly purchases of lands to keep it from being "developed" or farmed in ways that release pesticide run-offs. The alternative is for the city to spend as much as $5 billion for filtration systems to meet the federal government's Surface Water Treatment Rule.

When it comes to treating wastewater, estimates for getting New York into compliance with all wastewater and sewage regulations already on the books range from $50 billion and up—an impossibly large sum given the city's current and likely future fiscal circumstances.

Sludge treatment is the most pressing short-term problem involving sewage facing the city. Some 100 tons of New York sludge are now shipped daily to farmers in Colorado and Arizona as fertilizer. Additional facilities are being constructed in the Apple to turn even more of this messy material into valuable plant food. Because these new facilities will not be ready until the late 1990s, however, the city will have to spend $1.5 billion or so in coming years to ship sludge to processing plants in Virginia.

Still another new water-related enomic reality facing New Yorkers is water metering. City residents used to get their water for a flat rate, irrespective of real usage. Now, through metering, people will pay for the water they actually consume.

And what is the enomic result of this water toll collection for many low-income homeowners and low-end cooperative apartment owners? Today they face serious financial difficulties and even foreclosure proceedings.

The trend of charging urban dwellers by unit of waste produced by individuals, rather than meeting the costs of environmental protection via general taxation, goes beyond water. In places like Seattle, people have paid by the can to have their household trash removed for some years.

The problem with such a fee-for-services approach—at least in the minds of many tax critics—is that these fees are not collected by government in lieu of ordinary taxes but in addition to ordinary taxes. In response to New York officials who say that a fee is not a tax, these critics respond with the words of The Apple's most famous former mayor, Fiorello LaGuardia: "No matter how thin you slice it, it's still baloney."

Before leaving The Apple and its many environmental difficulties, one should also note some local enomic pluses.

Environmental management programs at New York University are attracting people from several surrounding states and may one day bring in well-heeled foreign students as well.

The New York publishing world is benefiting from sales of books about the environment. The New York trade and convention world is benefiting from the many green conferences and business get-togethers now held there. The Port of New York is benefiting from exports of recyclable waste such as newsprint and cardboard, which are now the Port's largest exports.

A hefty number of America's 600 venture capital firms, many of them looking with increasing favor at envirotech investments, are New York–based as well. Indeed, though the evidence is still spotty and largely anecdotal, it now seems certain that New York City is fast emerging as the capital font for America's enomic transformation.

Across the Hudson River from New York, the state of New Jersey is also moving to become a geographic enomic font of another sort. Governor Jim Florio, in his State of the State address in January 1993, announced plans to tie the economic revival of New Jersey to its role as leader in the envirotech revolution.

"Tomorrow, when people in Eastern Europe want to make the polluted Danube River blue again," Florio said, "when people in the Ukraine want to clean up Chernobyl, they will need environmental technology—and they will turn to New Jersey."

Looking around the country, there is perhaps no more striking example of how a regional economy is being transformed by environment-related considerations than California. To try to understand the current California economy (the *world's* sixth largest) without employing enomics measuring sticks would be roughly akin to ignoring the effects of the gold rush on a nascent California economy in the 1840s, or the combined effects of Hollywood, Silicon Valley, and the aerospace industry on California's post–World War II economic fortunes.

In terms of food raising, real estate valuations, new urban

and suburban development patterns, local tax burdens, the way people travel and the speed they get from place to place, the manner in which they earn their livelihoods, enomics more and more *is* California economics.

The state is already both a major center of the environmental cleanup industry and a national leader in generating ecoentrepreneurship. Located adjacent to Mexico and at the terminus of sea and air routes to Pacific Rim nations that require ever greater environmental services and ever more pollution control equipment, California is also emerging as this country's foremost exporter of many green goods.

To protect California air, automakers will have to sell 200,000 emission-free cars annually by the year 2003, a major challenge for the auto industry, and gasoline refiners will have to dramatically change their own products. Also to protect air quality, the state's major utilities will get most of their new energy from geothermal and other renewable sources during the balance of this decade.

In accordance with its very wide-ranging Proposition 65, a measure designed to restrict sale of toxic products within the state, Californians are obliging sellers of all sorts of goods to "go green" in order to do business there. This effort is affecting everything from what items appear on store shelves, to what cases appear on court dockets in a part of the United States notorious for the quantity of its environmental litigation.

California's huge agricultural sector, which was forced to cope with a six-year drought that only ended in the winter of 1992–93, continues to face enormous enomic competition for water from urban water users and local wildlife. New water allocation rules recently formulated by California's Water Resources Control Board show a definite bias toward urban dwellers and wildlife interests at the expense of farmers.

Other West Coast areas are experiencing their own enomic transformations. While the national media focus most often on old-forest loggers in Washington State as the victims of this process, pure and unpolluted air is considered one of the main reasons commercial real estate professionals in Spokane are thriving these days, while others in their field elsewhere in the country are in a deep recession.

Seattle, long known for its importance to the aerospace industry because it is headquarters of the Boeing Corporation, also has become in recent years the city that is arguably the single most concentrated center of American ecoentrepeneuring. It is a place where concern for the natural environment and small-business energy have combined with extraordinary intensity.

Another part of Washington State has achieved another kind of enomic significance. The old nuclear bomb-making facility on Hanford Reservation is filled with a lethal mix of nuclear and conventional wastes so mammoth, its dimensions have not yet been fully catalogued.

More than $500 million annually is now poured into the local economy around Hanford to help clean up this horror show from the Cold War, and the figure is expected to double in the not-too-distant future. Long-term damages to the Washington economy resulting from Hanford "leaks," however—whether these involve run-offs into fish spawning grounds or higher cancer treatment costs for people in the area—will exceed this windfall many times over.

Along with East Coast and West Coast cities and states, whole regions in between are seeing important portions of their economies contract or swell because of changing environmental imperatives. Water allocation is not just a concern peculiar to California. Throughout much of the American West and Southwest, it is perhaps the most visible manifestation of new enomic forces at work.

For much of this country's history, how to parcel out limited quantities of precious water in America's "Great Western Desert" has been *the* political issue in this region. Today, this always extraordinarily complex subject has a very pronounced enomic quality.

The need to protect wetlands, waterfowl, and fish such as salmon now blend with longtime conflicts for water among mining companies, farmers, and urban developers. The desire of tourist industry operators for unspoiled landscapes merge with the politics of irrigation (the last really important government subsidy for many western farmers), along with hydropower producers' own water requirements.

Along the Mexican border, American manufacturers seeking cheap business overhead compete for environmental rules that favor their own interests against those border town municipal officials who are worried about how to afford keeping their local air breathable and their local water drinkable.

In 1992 Congress passed a comprehensive measure favoring urban growth and wildlife preservation at the expense of some western farmers. A year earlier, however, most new real estate development had to be halted temporarily in Las Vegas because of a court decision that went in farmers' favor and deprived developers of water needed for their own projects.

In the latest rounds of the great water wars that will always be a feature of western politics and western life generally, the critical thing from the enomic perspective is not who wins or loses any given battle, but the overall direction the conflict is taking. Today the conflict is definitely becoming greener. Regional economics "out west" is becoming increasingly synonymous with regional enomics.

The human body is composed of many structures and systems. There are many centers of important functions, linked by neural and fluid networks. The interaction of these structures and systems, these centers and networks, make up a kind of physical romance of human existence. It is a romance that would be not only incomplete but impossible without organs that efficiently handle the wastes produced by any healthy organism.

The same kind of romance, of course, is now observable in human economies. The great discovery of late-twentieth-century economics is that proper neutralization or recycling of spent materials is every bit as important (if not quite as glamorous) as encouraging production or facilitating distribution. Creating wealth without concurrent waste control, we are finally coming to understand, is like inflating a very large balloon in a very small closet.

Good kidneys are every bit as vital to continued good health as a good heart. Renal failure can kill you as dead as heart failure. Similarly, in the new enomic geography, effective waste handling has become absolutely critical in keeping cities, states, and regions of the United States economically healthy and viable.

The next chapter discusses how enomic dramas are being played out on a larger geographic scale around the world. It links present and future economic success in the international marketplace with an intelligent application of the principles of a new environmental economics.

GOING GREEN
AROUND THE WORLD

In 1853 Commodore Matthew Perry entered Tokyo Harbor and forced an isolationist Japan to open itself up to western trade and western economic influences generally. The Japanese went on to master the technological and commercial techniques pioneered in the West so successfully, they are now the world's second greatest industrial power.

They did this, however, without becoming "a western nation." Japan remains an Asian nation. The first fully industrialized Asian nation.

In 1979 the Ayatollah Ruholla Khomeini led a revolution in Iran that toppled the Shah and replaced his government with a theocratic Islamic republic. In spite of a devastating eight-year war with Iraq, attempts by the United States and other nations to restrict its access to various technologies, and "reforms" to the national banking and commercial system that many predicted would be crippling, Iran today is making very rapid progress toward becoming a modern economic power.

But again, this process is not making the country "a western nation" in any real sense. The Iranian road to technological modernity is a peculiarly Iranian one.

What these two examples illustrate is that profound economic transformations not only can occur in different ways within different cultural matrices, they invariably do occur in a very nation-specific, culture-specific manner. In just the way that "going modern" economically (moving from poorer agricultural dependence to a richer industrial status) does not happen in a uniform way, "going green" enomically (entering into this next phase of the Industrial Revolution) occurs at different speeds and in different ways depending on the nature of the society in which the phenomenon takes place.

This reality, of course, represents a serious conundrum for some environmental thinkers who have finally mustered the scientific data to justify ecology-oriented economic actions. These people now face new frustrations in trying to push through perfectly logical, perfectly consistent environmental economic agendas on governments and societies whose operations are totally illogical (except from the standpoint of their own historical circumstances) and altogether inconsistent with the uniform lending and aid standards favored by World Bank and United Nations one-world pundits.

This is not to say that no international or transnational agreements or treaties are relevant when it comes to understanding the Enomic Revolution as it affects various countries. Quite the contrary.

Measures such as the 1975 Convention on International Trade in Endangered Species, the 1987 Montreal Protocol concerning the phaseout of chlorofluorocarbons, and several other international treaties, are certainly changing the way many national economies function. Quasi-treaties, such as "Agenda 21," a kind of wish list for environmental improvement that emerged from the 1992 U.N. earth summit in Rio de Janeiro, Brazil, are also having an effect.

Transnational regional agreements concerning the environment are playing even more important roles in bringing about international enomic change. The green sections of the North American Free Tree Agreement (NAFTA) and the many European Community (EC) agreements on environmental protection amply demonstrate as much.

Overall, however, just as the axiom "all aspects of the new environmental economics have a distinctive local flavor" made sense within our last chapter's purely American context, it makes equal sense when viewing enomic changes around the world. This will remain true even as the more internationalist, pro-environmental bent of a new Clinton White House makes itself felt.

Hence the need for Americans to understand comparative enomics—the ways in which other nations, other societies, are meeting or failing to meet new environmental economic imperatives. As enomics becomes an increasingly vital element of the world economic system of which we are a part, understanding enomics becomes ever more critical in positioning ourselves to remain internationally competitive.

Studying comparative enomic transformations also offers positive insights from which Americans can learn, and horrendous negative examples of what can happen when enomic lessons are not learned. It offers clues about the likely political futures of places like Eastern Europe as well. Indeed, in a very fundamental way, an international enomic vision is the mechanism that most clearly reveals, for better or worse, the nature of the "new world order" President Bush so loudly proclaimed and so thoroughly failed to define.

Japan's industrialization began almost a century later than Great Britain's. Shortly after Admiral Perry's fleet forced a very reluctant feudal country to open its doors to the outside world, Japan began willingly and aggressively to import and employ Western expertise and technologies during the 1860s.

The shorthand for this process, which was applicable until relatively recently when the Japanese became world-class industrial innovators in their own right, was "adopt, adapt, adept." So well and fast did Japan follow this precept that by 1905 it was able to defeat in the Russo-Japanese War a country that was at least nominally "Western."

Though rich in the talent and the enterprise of its people, Japan is very poor in terms of natural resources, especially petroleum. This paucity has been very important in shaping

Japanese industrial history. As David Halberstam noted in his book, *The Next Century* (1991): "There was nothing very ideological about Japanese capitalism. ... Everything was based on the best use of the nation's limited resources."

By the 1930s, a combination of this resource poverty, the worldwide recession, and a ferocious chauvinist-based militarization had reduced many Japanese to the brink of starvation. The nation's total defeat in World War II only increased its desperate situation.

Between 1945 and 1970, Japan recovered and rapidly modernized its industrial base. One of the major victims of this modernization, however, was the island nation's own territorial ecosystems and surrounding waters.

While there has always been an indigenous reverence for nature among the Japanese, it has been tempered by adversarial feelings, too, a sense of nature as bringer of hardship as well as provider. Pro-environment sentiments here were thus far less important in determining national priorities in the post–World War II period than a consensus-driven determination to overcome long years of poverty and the industrial inferiority felt in those years by most Japanese.

By the time the 1960s rolled around, no Japanese equivalent of a Rachel Carson was around to inspire an alienated and pampered middle-class youth to reject materialism in favor of a nature-based, improved "quality of life." The nation's total energies were tightly focused on catching up, first with leading industrial powers in Western Europe (which was accomplished by 1968), then with the United States.

The obvious way to accomplish this end *seemed* to be to accept very high levels of local air, water, and soil contamination. And geographical factors greatly magnified the pollution consequences of this mistaken approach. According to a 1985 Congressional Budget Office publication called *Environmental Regulation and Economic Efficiency*:

> Japan has perhaps the most consistently "unforgiving" natural environment. Most of its terrain is mountainous, and the amount of habitable land is

small as a percentage of the total. As a result, Japan
is a highly urbanized country (80 percent of its population lives in cities), with high population densities
(744 per square mile) and industrial development
within urban centers. Such topography and growth
compound the task of achieving acceptable environmental quality within these areas.

The upshot of Japan's enomics-hostile economic policies
as they combined with its geographic circumstances were as
tragic as they were inevitable. In the 1960s people in large
industrial cities such as Tokyo were obliged to walk around
wearing gauze masks because of polluted air. Forests were
dying. Lakes throughout the country had become highly acidic
and otherwise toxic.

Using the straight-line method for disposing of industrial
wastes available to any island nation, the Japanese had built
most of their factories near the shore and simply dumped dangerous chemicals into the water. Untreated. By the late 1960s
thousands of people in this country where fish is the traditional
protein staple started sickening due to mercury poisoning (Mi-
namata disease), PCB poisoning, chrome poisoning, and industrial ills for which no name has been assigned to this day.

Finally, these very unpleasant realities produced a new
mood within the country. In 1970—a very significant year in
the enomic history of both Japan and the United States—
national policies concerning health and industrial production
underwent an intensive reevaluation. A changed consensus regarding the environment and the economy jelled within the
government-industrial combine running Japan.

This consensus found concrete expression in actions of
the so-called Environmental Diet session of the Japanese parlia-
ment, which passed fourteen major laws with enormous
ecological and economic implications. These included establishment of a national Environmental Agency, passage of the
only measure in any industrial nation requiring compensation
for victims of industrial pollution, and a tax bill called "The
Law Concerning Enterprise Burden-Sharing," which forced Japa-

nese companies to pay a share of the costs of their own polluting practices.

So successful was this latter law that by the mid-1970s, Japanese firms were spending twice as much on pollution control on average as their American counterparts. "External" environmental costs, which were formerly ignored by society altogether or borne totally by government, started to be partially "internalized" within company budgets—a process that also was beginning in the United States in this same period via regulation policy rather than tax policy.

While these approaches toward checking pollution had few detractors, some other practices instituted by the Japanese in the early 1970s were to raise the hackles of foreign critics in later years. One practice in particular attracted increasing hostility: Japanese *exports* of dangerous wastes.

Other industrial nations, of course, were doing the same thing at almost exactly the same time. Americans sent some of their toxic waste output (and much more of their toxic production) south to Mexico. The French and Italians sent it to old colonies in Africa. Germans sent it to the Communist-run eastern part of their own country—an amazingly bad choice, as it turned out, because after national reunification in 1990, in the best Hermann Hesse "what-goes-around, comes-around" tradition, the problem came back to them in the form of monumentally expensive remediation problems.

The Japanese, for their part, initiated huge exports of toxic waste, mostly to less developed nations in Southeast Asia. At the same time they were starting to employ far less destructive techniques in harvesting their own forests, they also began using heavily forested parts of Asia, Amazonia, and the northwestern United States to meet their huge needs for timber to service a domestic construction boom.

During the decade of the 1970s, the Japanese pursued one other new policy line as well—one rather more favorably enomic in nature, and one with the potential to be both economically sound in the short term and ecologically sustainable over a longer period. They began to manufacture goods in a way that was less materially wasteful, less polluting, and more efficient. To a deeply rooted Japanese "waste-nothing" ethic was added the caveat "waste nothing and release no dangerous waste."

This process accelerated sharply after 1974, the year Saudi Arabia led the Organization of Petroleum Exporting Countries (OPEC) in precipitating the world's first great oil supply crisis. Every industrial nation felt the jolt, but the Japanese, with almost no domestic petroleum supplies of the kind possessed by both the United States and Western Europe (with its North Sea reserves), and therefore dependent on Middle Eastern sources to meet the vast majority of its energy needs, were severely jolted.

American officials in the 1970s still had enough economic leeway to dither about whether to institute enomic measures such as national conservation. So dither they did. During the Carter administration, a new cabinet-level agency called the Department of Energy did little more than agonize over "defining a mission."

In Japan, meanwhile, the powers-that-be were obliged to take much quicker and more decisive actions. They focused on national conservation aimed at making their country's industries and transportation networks more efficient, more technically advanced, and less dependent on costly oil imports.

One result of this effort (piggybacked as it was on the impetus to release less dangerous and domestically destructive wastes) was that Japan became more internationally competitive because it got more goods per kilowatt of energy and per pound of raw material. An equally important spinoff of these policies was the improvement of the nation's own environmental quality.

There is thus a curious inversion of causes and effects to be seen in the enomic roads followed by Americans and Japanese. "The environment" was America's chief industrial policy in years after 1970, in that it obliged American manufacturers to be less polluting, less wasteful, hence more competitive. "The economy," meanwhile, was Japan's chief environmental policy in this same period, in that it forced Japanese manufacturers to be less wasteful, hence less polluting.

Both histories, of course, bring us back to our two core enomic equations:

What's good for the environment = What's good for the economy

and

What's good for the economy = What's good for the environment

Not surprisingly, there was some backsliding on Japan's road to enomics. "Inspired," as it were, by the Reagan administration's utter disdain for environmental protection and total lack of enomic understanding, the Japanese slowed their own enomic efforts in the early 1980s. A huge increase in the number of diesel-powered vehicles on its highways also contributed to a deterioration of air quality in Tokyo and other major Japanese cities after 1987.

A second enomic wave, however, began sweeping through the country's economy by the start of the 1990s. It was triggered by new worldwide fears about environmental health, raising consciousness spawned by the Rio conference, and, most important, a renewed and much-strengthened national appreciation of the linkage between environmentally sound practices and economic expediency.

The current enomic policies of Japan present a striking combination of very desirable and highly questionable lessons for public and corporate policymakers in the United States and elsewhere. Perhaps the element most worth emulating is the very comprehensive nature of Japan's approaches to new environmental economic challenges and opportunities.

The Japanese are playing the enomic game much like they play their national board game, Go. Instead of quick advantages or individual victories involving a few "pieces," they are flowing in a greener direction around the board with the obvious intention of achieving victory through strategic envelopments. Their chief international opponent in the world economic sweepstakes, the United States, meanwhile, has been playing enomics (at least at the governmental level) like a schoolyard checkers match.

There are useful things to learn from Japanese administrative enomics, too, which is very different from that of the United States. The Japan Environment Agency, for example, is not a powerful policy instrument operated largely to advance the views and interests of environmentalists. It is a relatively weak agency that tends to cooperate with industry when it comes to setting environmental standards—working to bring about consensus rather than confrontation.

The really important government initiatives in melding environmental and economic policies come from the Ministry of International Trade and Industry (MITI). Such a bureaucratic arrangement in and of itself firmly establishes "the environment" within an official economic and technology-based policy context.

It was MITI that in the early 1990s announced a "New Earth 21" plan designed to merge Japanese economic growth and worldwide environmental protection during the twenty-first century. This agency's energy-saving budget was boosted 55 percent for fiscal 1993 alone, a year in which it will spend more than $2 billion of the $7.7 billion in "green aid" announced by the Japanese at the 1992 Rio earth summit.

MITI's $2.4 billion "Eco-Phoenix Plan" is a kind of pilot program to help ten to fifteen cities in different parts of the world reduce their carbon dioxide emissions. Its "New Sunshine Project" will run through the year 2020 and spend upward of $13 billion to help boost the efficiency technologies employed by Japanese companies.

The agency is building the world's first facility devoted exclusively to developing ecology-saving techniques, the Research Institute of Innovative Technology for the Earth. It also plans to "encourage" more than two thousand Japanese service stations to sell alternative fuels and electricity to power cars by the year 2000.

The work of other organs of Japanese government are neatly integrated into this MITI-led national enomic effort. The Foreign Ministry, for example, has approximately $400 million budgeted in 1993 to export green technology.

The billions of dollars' worth of green foreign aid coming

from various Japanese government organs these days for air pollution control, reforestation, and water purification projects serve the enomic ends of Japanese policy in securing future economic leverage in many parts of the world, as well as winning the country new respect in international environmental circles. Indeed, the Japanese can be said to be "Bechtel-ing" us when it comes to using the environment to further their own economic goals.

U.S. design and engineering firms first got an infrastructure business foothold in developing nations during the 1950s and 1960s by building naval facilities and airfields funded by U.S. government Cold War military aid. The Japanese are today establishing similar footholds in developing countries for future environmental infrastructure projects with their own green aid programs.

Such a pattern, of course, is familiar to every student of modern economic history. The Japanese are doing to us today when it comes to environmental (and quite a number of other) technologies pretty much what we did to the British earlier in this century. Britain's scientists and inventors created new techniques and devices. American businesspeople commercialized them, sold them around the world, and took home most of the jobs and profits.

There is certainly no shortage of opportunities for the Japanese to do the same thing when it comes to peddling green goods in years to come. Just in Asia, there are undeveloped nations where green aid today will mean green technology orders tomorrow, as well as more economically advanced states in other parts of the world ready to make heavy purchases of green goods from suppliers like Japan.

Hong Kong, for example, is an island with millions of people and almost no wastewater treatment facilities (other than the surrounding Pacific Ocean). The once-exquisite forests of Thailand are today very heavily damaged, as are huge tracts of wooded areas in the Philippines. Nations such as South Korea have created First World production systems while operating Third World environmental protection infrastructures. And China, which derives three-quarters of its energy from mostly low-quality brown coal, and where a "development comes first" official attitude prevails, currently endures some of the world's worst air pollution.

Taiwan, however, a former Japanese colony, demonstrates most clearly how a progressive enomic exporter of green goods moves to seize opportunities. In 1991 Taiwan announced a six-year $300 billion program to upgrade its island infrastructure. Much of this spending will go into water and sewage treatment facilities, because in some Taiwanese provinces, only 1 or 2 percent of the wastewater is currently treated.

The United States is Taiwan's biggest foreign customer. For that reason, the United States should be first in line to receive a substantial portion of that island's green-tech orders. To cash in such a market, however, requires a policy to funnel trade in the direction of America's own green industry.

For many years the U.S. government had no such policy. The Japanese government did. In consequence, according to some private estimates, Japanese green goods sellers now fill 85 percent of Taiwan's green goods needs, while the United States and other suppliers divide up the remaining 15 percent.

Other elements of the Japanese government's comprehensive domestic and international enomic planning include a five-year program to spend $617 billion on improving highways and reducing vehicular pollution, and the Ministry of Agriculture, Forestry and Fisheries' plan to create an environmental research center to help other nations combat erosion and other soil-related problems. The Environmental Agency also, through its "Global Environmental Fund," will funnel billions of dollars to Japanese firms to help them with such projects as establishing a network of Japanese-run recycling facilities to process foreign wastes.

As part of the coordinated national effort to go enomic, the private sector of the Japanese economy is naturally as important as its government counterpart. According to a report in the *Wall Street Journal*, "some 40 percent of Japan's largest industrial companies have now [by 1990] established their in-house environmental divisions."

These include giants such as Canon, Hitachi, Kawasaki

Heavy Industries, Sumitomo Metal, and Tokyo Electric. Fuji Electric is among the Japanese heavyweights positioning themselves to garner huge pieces of the Enomic Revolution's burgeoning earth-safe energy business by becoming a leader in fuel cell development. Overall, by 1991, Japanese papermakers derived half their feedstock from used paper, steelmakers recycled four-fifths of their manufacturing waste, and textile producers recycled more than half their own wastes.

Japanese carmakers have long been enomically progressive. Catalytic converters were part of Japan's export models as early as 1975. One hint that Japanese auto companies intend to remain in the enomic vanguard in future years comes from a recent report issued by the Environmental Agency. "Research into combustion," it notes, "has advanced and Japanese cars now meet the most stringent exhaust emissions standards . . . [and have] the greatest combustion efficiencies in the world."

Other indications of how Japanese car manufacturers are seeking to keep their green edge include electric car prototypes now coming from Toyota and Nissan. Mazda's hydrogen fuel concept car, introduced at the very end of 1992, is another harbinger here.

It would be a very serious mistake to equate the undeniable intelligence and energy now going into Japan's public and industrial enomic policies with a universal prescription for what every nation ought to do in this realm, however. With respect to the United States, in fact, there are most certainly things here we should *not* seek to emulate.

Japan's generic attitude toward nature (something to be reconfigured into usefulness) and its definition of pollution (a social nuisance) fill many American environmentalists, quite rightly, with despair. Some current government and corporate "enomic" planning in Japan also is not only grandiose to the point of *hubris*, but actually qualifies as anti-enomic in the sense that quantities of energy and materials needed to construct proposed projects like huge solar power stations in out-of-the-way deserts make such schemes potentially very earth-unfriendly.

It is exactly in the field of meeting future energy needs,

in fact, that the worst negative examples of Japanese enomic thinking are to be found. Here, the inherent limitations of a national consensus approach toward solving problems, as opposed to the American slugfest approach to similar challenges, are most in evidence.

In 1966, Japan embarked on a huge program to replace much of its oil imports used to produce 80 percent of its power with locally produced nuclear fuel. The core of this effort was to be breeder reactors, turning nuclear waste into plutonium, which in turn would fuel more power production.

After a quarter of a century and $5 billion in costs on a breeder facility, the plutonium program, and with it a major component of the country's entire long-term energy strategy, is in jeopardy. "Monju," the name given the proposed Japanese breeder, is in technical straits and may never be completed. Nuclear waste must therefore be shipped to France to be turned into plutonium.

The world is up in arms about the ecological and terrorist threats posed by these shipments. The cost of plutonium-generated electricity produced without a domestic breeder reactor is also increasingly uncompetitive compared to nonnuclear power.

Japan got into its present plutonium bind in large measure because in a consensus-based society, once "everyone" reaches a decision, everyone goes along. Because a few people would not go along in the United States, this country eventually abandoned its own deeply flawed breeder program in the late 1970s.

What, then, should Americans learn, and not learn, about enomics from our prime world economic rival, the Japanese? In the field of energy, the lesson is to always lean toward options that are least susceptible to technological obsolescence, supply disruptions, or nasty down-the-road health discoveries.

This option today is conservation and increased efficiency. Because the United States is now so far behind the Japanese when it comes to conservation and efficiency, *this* is where the biggest rewards for the fewest bucks can most quickly be realized.

In a more generic vein, the key positive enomic lesson the Japanese have to teach is the value of government environmental economic policies that are consistent, comprehensive, and uniformly supportive of enomic objectives promoting greater efficiency within a national economy while boosting exports. The key negative enomic lesson is that while less confrontation between business and environmental groups is certainly desirable, it must be achieved without silencing, or ignoring, those pesky, feisty voices from below that not infrequently see the world more sensible than the grandees on the heights.

If Japan and the United States followed different roads in moving toward the same enomic ends, czarist Russia, its successor the Soviet Union, and that Union's own successor states went off on a different track altogether.

Peter the Great is usually credited with turning the eyes of Russia westward in the early eighteenth century. This process included laying the foundation for industrialization, but it was a foundation that proved anemic by the standards of Great Britain and Germany during the next 150 years.

Industrial capitalism really began to take hold in Russia only at the end of the nineteenth century. By then, prior acquisition and settling of Siberia in the east had made the country vast, while additional conquest of lands in Central Asia, equal in size to half the continental United States, had turned it into an empire.

The very size of this empire made Russia's industrialization spotty and less of a defining economic (or ecological) force than was the case in the far smaller states of Western Europe. The lack of a commitment to genuine modernization among Russia's still largely feudal rulers also kept this industrialization from being as complete and successful as the one in a formerly feudal Japan.

The Communists came to power in 1917. Their revolution disdained nature as did all nineteenth-century "progress" ideologies. This disdain was only intensified by a fixation with gigantivism (especially as it applied to hydroelectric projects), which was the pet fetish of the revolution's leader, Vladimir I. Lenin. It was a combination that boded ill for the Soviet Union's ecosystems in the following years.

If pre-enomics industrial and agricultural development in the Soviet Union was singularly insulated from even the modest environmentalist restraints prevailing in the United States during the 1920s and 1930s (restraints such as zoning laws and a weak but persistent nature lobby), at least most of this development was contained within the long-settled western lands of the country and its Caucasian oil fields. The coming of World War II changed this picture dramatically.

Whole industries moved east ahead of the advancing German armies. When the war ended, new or vastly expanded industrial centers in the Ural Mountains and farther east rivaled their western sister-cities in an ability to produce pollution as well as manufactured goods.

Again, as was the case with the United States and Japan, the early 1970s were critical in the enomic history of the Soviet Union. Unlike the United States, however, which began to make enomic progress because of spreading ecological awareness, or Japan, which did the same to quickly accommodate new economic necessities, enomic evolution in the Soviet Union in the 1970s never got off the ground.

There was no legally recognized or even permitted environmental lobby, because most opposition to the destruction of the Union's ecosystems was identified with a "nationalities question" the Soviet authorities chose to consider no longer relevant. And while the very best government economists of the period did see a need to modernize industry and agriculture in ways that also would have had beneficial ecological consequences, the country's leaders ignored these suggestions.

Why? Because to act upon them would have required displacing entrenched party managers and caused unemployment among some sectors of the industrial work force—not to mention exposing glaring errors in official state political and economic doctrine.

The 1970s enomic challenge in the United States and Japan was a threat to certain established interests. In the Soviet

Union, it was a threat to the system itself. In a very fundamental sense, it was treason, and was regarded as such.

Preserving this system through more of the same rather than through timely implementation of a few radical innovations was the primary enomic response of the Soviet Union between 1970 and its dissolution in 1990. The pattern here was almost exactly analogous to the failure of Russian aristocrats to come to grips with the imperatives of a modern industrial economy between the emancipation of the serfs in 1861 and the 1917 revolution.

To phrase this another way: Russia, unlike Japan, missed the boat during the first stage of its Industrial Revolution. Then, unlike Japan, it missed the boat again during the second enomic stage of this vast ecological-economic drama.

Some national leaderships never seem to evolve. And their people always pay the price.

Perhaps the defining example of late Soviet-style enomic idiocy involved attempts to irrigate lands around the 26,000-square-mile Aral Sea in the Central Asian part of the old Soviet Union. The project was totally pre-enomic in conception and purely Soviet in execution.

It completely ignored environmental considerations in an attempt to realize economic benefits. As a result, both the ecology and the wealth-producing potential of the sea itself were destroyed, as was the potentially cotton-rich acreage around that body of water.

The Aral Sea tragedy was one of countless, unconnected, anti-enomic incidents that characterized Soviet planning for decades. Along with these sporadic episodes, Soviet officials engaged in a systematic, determined, profoundly anti-enomic misuse of nuclear power, for purely ideological reasons as part of the new Soviet man's unrelenting war on natural man.

As surely as electrification was communism (to paraphrase the words of Lenin) in the 1920s and 1930s, nuclear power was communism in the 1950s through 1980s. It was "modern." It smacked of "progress." It was able to produce "showpieces." If one was not overly bothered by the occasional nuclear experiment run amok in Ukraine or the Urals, or by the dumping of thousands of tons of highly radioactive wastes in Arctic waters, or by a Chernobyl-like incident or two (provided it could be hushed up), it was a system that even seemed to be "successful."

Such success was copiously exported to the Soviet Union's Eastern European satellites during the Cold War years. Today, some sixty Soviet-built nuclear power plants in this region are deemed potentially dangerous. Fifteen of these have designs similar to the facility at Chernobyl. Two in Lithuania and one in Bulgaria are widely viewed as very dangerous—but neither can be closed down immediately because local economies have become so dependent on their continued operation.

Costs to replace these plants totally with safer generating facilities may run as high as $100 billion. Just to get the most dangerous ones off-line or even rendered "relatively safe" will require $9 billion to $12 billion, which may or may not be forthcoming from EC or U.S. sources in the next few years.

Not enough time has elapsed since the anti-Soviet revolutions that swept Eastern Europe in 1989 and the one that brought down the Soviet Union itself in 1990 for a full catalog of communism's enomic costs to emerge. In a report prepared for the Worldwatch Institute as early as 1990, however, it was estimated that environmental damage was costing Poland as much as 20 percent of its annual gross national product and Czechoslovakia as much as 7 percent of its GNP.

Corollary enomic costs reflected in health care spending, along with potential productivity losses related to living in places with mind-numbing ecological damages, are only now being reported by the United Nations, the new Russian government, and a host of private sources. Environmental damages, for example, are contributing significantly to the near collapse of national health care systems in Russia and Ukraine. Children in particular are being affected by bad air, water, and other contaminants, to the point where only about one-quarter of those leaving school today in these republics are classified as "healthy."

The current reintroduction of capitalism and a market economy into the life of former Soviet Union states is not, unfortunately, necessarily the solution to many enomic problems. In the short run, in fact, such restructuring may make things worse by opening up some formerly undeveloped lands to "development" and by replacing a rather highly evolved recycling system for some packaging with a 1950s-style throwaway mentality that many East Europeans have come to associate with a new capitalistic era.

Even more basic, the current transition to a market economy is destroying a set of Communist values (outmoded and discredited though they may be) and the spiritual values of Eastern Europeans that had ameliorated at least some of communism's banality and hypocrisy. It is substituting a vulgarized and often blatantly exploitative Dickensian capitalism now identified in Eastern Europe with international Mafia and banking interests.

The way enomics, the new environmental economics, ultimately finds political as well as economic expression in this part of the world may well horrify many liberal environmentalists who identify an imperative to protect and restore natural ecologies with international brotherhood and evolved feelings toward living creatures generally. There are, alas, other less attractive ways to bring about enomic ends. These involve substituting chauvinist enterprise and folk passions for capital and high technology.

One sees, in fact, an eerie resonance between the racist rhetoric of national purification so prevalent in the Mittel-Europa of the 1930s and the nationalist environmental regeneration rhetoric now circulating within post-Soviet Eastern Europe. No one with an understanding of twentieth-century history in this region and an acquaintance with the area's current economic and ecological realities discounts the possible emergence of ecofascism here.

Just as Americans have much to learn from the Japanese enomic model, we have much to learn from the Soviet Union's experience. If the enomic credo in the United States today is "You can have it all," its *doppelgänger* in Eastern Europe is that "You can also end up with nothing at all."

To American critics of a new environmental economics

who say there is no proof that environmental deterioration poses an immediate threat to our way of life, to people who still believe that economies are benefited rather than destroyed by polluting practices, one need only point to countries of the former Soviet Bloc. In Poland, more than 60 percent of the water is unsafe to drink. In northern Bohemia, the average life span of industrial workers is declining. In Ukraine, where sickness among children and a nation's dimming economic future are clearly linked by the agency of environmental contamination.

These are the things to come of any nation which in one way or another does not meet the enomic challenge.

The enomic approaches of countries other than Japan and the old Soviet Union hold considerable interest for American business and government planners—even if they have less direct importance as positive or negative models to be followed or avoided. Consider, in this regard, the recent enomic history of Mexico.

Mexico's first experience with significant infusions of foreign capital came at the start of this century. It took the form of North Americans and Europeans seeking cheap factory labor and access to huge mineral wealth. Mexico's 1917 revolution was a strongly nationalist event due, in part, to hostility toward these foreign interests.

The revolution turned the country economically inward for decades. In so doing, it helped keep Mexico economically poorer but environmentally "unspoiled" until the oil shocks of the 1970s.

A few boom years followed on the heels of the Arab oil embargo because of Mexico's own huge, state-owned oil reserves. The boom spurred a taste for consumer goods among a suddenly ballooning middle class. It also precipitated a considerable amount of environmental deterioration, the natural product of a swollen, badly run oil industry.

By the 1980s, premium prices were no longer being paid for petroleum. The residual production-linked environmental damages did not disappear, however. To this damage was gradually added huge amounts of air pollution inundating the capital and manufacturing hub, Mexico City, and widespread water pollution generated by maquiladoras (assembly plants) in its newly industrialized northern tier of states.

By the early 1990s the Mexican economy was ripe to take on a new enomic orientation, because the country's leadership realized that failure to do so threatened political stability as well as recent economic progress. Average per capita income in Mexico had risen to $3,458 by 1992, abysmal by American standards where the comparable income was $22,690, but well above Mexican incomes just a few years earlier.

Much of this increased personal income was tied to trade with the rest of the world, which totaled $104 billion in 1991. Trade with Canada and the United States has grown 15 to 20 percent in recent years, and combined exports and imports with the United States alone totaled $71 billion by 1991.

Continued expansion of this trade-based economic growth through approval of a North American Free Trade Agreement (NAFTA) and other international pacts, however, became closely tied to remediation of environmental horrors inflicted by a very rapid and badly managed industrialization. The United States, an unwilling recipient of many of Mexico's least desirable "pollution exports" along their 2000-mile joint border, pressed very hard to have its southern neighbor clean up its enomic act.

Mexico's announcement in early 1992 that it would spend $4 billion in the following two years to reduce air pollution was one of many "official" responses to such pressure. The World Bank's announcement later in the year that it would lend Mexico more than $200 million for environmental cleanup gave substance to this intent. The Mexican government's plan to boost environmental spending 27 percent in its 1993 budget was still another straw in the enomic wind.

The *real* impetus for enomic change in Mexico, however, came not from abroad and not from government, but from the country's own best-educated and well-to-do citizens. And herein lies another interesting and important fact about enomics as it is being played out in countries still not yet fully developed economically but well along on that path—the true meaning of *"sustainability"* as it applies to the study of enomics.

Sustainability, in fact, turns out to be not so much a biological limitation on overall economic expansion (at least in the near term), as postulated by some environmental theorists, so much as a class squeal of pain from the *nouveau riche* seeking to brake a certain type of economic expansion. Certainly, this is the way of things in Mexico.

Half of the country's 85 million people still live in dire poverty. This underclass is applying little or no political pressure to check pollution. Nor are low-paid Mexican factory and municipal workers leading the domestic charge against poor enomic policies. They too are by and large willing to "sustain" exposure to a great deal more concentrated pollution if it seems necessary to keep a job.

It is the newly enriched Mexican middle class that finds the country's current pollution levels unsustainable. This is the group that views a deteriorating environment as a direct challenge to its own recently realized sense of finally achieving the good life.

A bank manager in Mexico City leaves his pleasant residence and walks the few steps to his brand-new automobile. Along the way he is forced to breathe air so foul that schools are sometimes closed to protect children from going outside, thousands of factories are ordered shut to reduce pollution levels, and people feed coins into machines that sell them a few puffs of certified clean air.

Confronting such local Mexico City atmospherics, arguably the worst urban air in the world, this manager thinks: "I went to Harvard. I drive a Mercedes. I shouldn't have to breathe this!"

Of such domestically spawned, psychologically induced social perceptions are enomically sound national policies being created throughout the fastest-growing and most dynamic parts of the developing world. This Mexican middle-class reaction is being replicated in emerging economies stretching from the rest of Latin America to the tigers of Asia.

In Seoul, South Korea, the city with the world's highest per capita density of Ph.D.s in a land with some of the world's most polluted waterways, members of a newly enlarged middle class are also bumping up against the psychological sustainability barrier while contemplating the liquid coming out of their water taps.

A highly educated Korean today thinks: "I'm a doctor. My country will soon be united. We will then surpass our old occupier, Japan, in wealth and efficiency. I shouldn't have to drink *this*!"

Similar thoughts are occurring farther south, in Taiwan, which has its own very serious air and water pollution problems. There a young professional thinks: "My country has the world's largest hard currency reserves. Since the 1950s, we have made miraculous economic progress against incredible odds. I shouldn't have to drink or breathe *this*!"

Just as the primary engine driving new enomic policies among Asia's tigers and in other fast-developing nations around the world are internal, the same is true in still largely underdeveloped nations of the Third World—though with market forces not fully operative in many of these places, enomic progress there is still relatively slow.

In the late 1950s through 1980s, many poor countries such as Angola, Ethiopia, and Cuba set out to "punish" the West by going Communist. They ended up punishing only themselves.

Countries that today attempt an updated, environmentalist version of this Third World Aid Hustle will not "punish" developed countries in any meaningful way through relatively minor additions to worldwide atmospheric degradation, either. They will only punish their own people and undermine in fairly short order their own indigenous economies.

An increasing number of Third World leaders are coming to recognize this fact. They are less and less inclined to define economic "growth" the way it was defined in the 1950s, when growth was synonymous with more smokestacks, more conversion of raw materials into finished goods any way you can do it, and inevitably, more pollution.

In a world where there is a huge over-supply of manufactured goods such as cars and televisions, why try to become yet another competitor in car and TV markets? In a world where services rather than product manufacture are more and more what creates new wealth, the most intelligent Third World economic leaders are focusing their efforts on non-smokestack (and only limited mining and timbering) roads to growth.

One sees this in the exceptionally intelligent ecotourism programs of Costa Rica and the occasionally well-managed ecotourism program of Kenya. Until recently, it was also apparent in the way Beirut functioned as a low-pollution (and thus enomic) banking center and pleasure preserve for much of the Mideast and the way at least part of Uruguay's natural environment was saved from undue pollution because of that country's role as a tax haven for Argentinians.

The best thinkers in the Third World are no longer interested in caging a few crumbs from their richer neighbors. They are loathe to engage in economic growth spasms built on excessive pollution, which inevitably lead in very short order to monstrous economic and ecological hangovers.

Instead, they are working to build a now and future enomic basis for long-term wealth. They have stopped *Waiting For Lefty* by looking to Marxism for economic models. They have learned the futility of *Waiting for Godot* in the form of megaproject World Bank assistance.

Germany, like Japan, has historically exhibited a combination of very progressive enomic policies domestically and some very nasty enomic policies with respect to other countries. One major difference between Germany and Japan in this regard today, however, is that one of the "other countries" environmentally victimized by the old Federal Republic of Germany was reunited with that nation in 1990. Another major difference is that the enomics of present-day reunited Germany is being greatly shaped by rules of a transnational association (the European Community), rather than the more nebulous pressures of world opinion working to reshape some of Japan's own policies.

With respect to purely domestic enomics, the old West Germany's first "Federal Environmental Program" became law in 1971. It was supplemented a few years later by two highly successful tax measures, the Waste Water Law and the Water Management Law, which mandated payments by polluting companies of "user fees," whose size depended on the toxicity of a company's discharges.

A similar approach that involved taxing automobiles based on their emissions became law in 1985. A short while later, another auto-related measure required car manufacturers to take back and recycle their products when these vehicles' driving days were done.

Measures like these, of course, have made German car exports environmentally kind and thus more enomically salable. Plans by German manufacturers to use bar-codes on parts to aid vehicle disassembly will naturally increase their cars' enomic worth further, particularly in environmentally hypersensitive markets such as California.

Overall, according to the German Economic Institute, a reunited Germany now spends 1.7 percent of its GNP on pollution control and cleanup, second in the world only to Austria, which spends 1.9 percent. (The comparable figure for the United States is 1.4 percent and for Japan 1.08 percent.) Because almost two-thirds of this spending is by private companies rather than government, incentives to become less polluting and less wasteful have made German firms (in the best enomic tradition) far more internationally competitive in recent years.

At the Rio conference in June 1992, Germany's announcement that it would reduce carbon dioxide emissions 25 percent by the year 2005 from 1987 levels was greeted by the Bush administration as a sign of overzealous environmentalism. In fact, it was merely an expression of a new efficiency-cum-competitive enomic way of thinking among German industrialists.

Certain other aspects of the new enomics are less favorable for a recently enlarged Germany. Between now and the year 2000, the country will have to spend at least $120 billion to clean up its eastern territories, much of whose enormous environmental damages occurred because of toxic waste exports from West Germany.

This expression of the law of enomic returns is one of the chief reasons Germany's economic growth has slowed since 1990. A huge Baltic Sea cleanup program, weening the old East Germany from dependence on the highly polluting brown coal that used to provide 70 percent of its total energy, the closing down and replacing of Soviet-era nuclear facilities, and the remediating of slurries left over from a huge uranium mining program East Germany operated at the behest of the Soviet Union have all contributed to making the long hoped for national reunification a less happy event than anticipated.

Germany still ships huge amounts of wastes abroad. These take the form of both nontoxic municipal solid waste and more toxic varieties. The country is the world's biggest garbage exporter, according to the *Wall Street Journal*, sending 557,000 tons of trash annually to other nations of Western Europe, most notably to landfills in France.

This practice may soon end, however. While most trade barriers came down for EC countries at the start of 1993, a prior ruling by EC officials held that this open-borders policy did *not* cover the right of one community member to restrict garbage imports from other members after 1993. Such a policy only hastens Germany's already very serious efforts toward greener packaging and overall recycling to reduce solid waste.

Germany has already passed very stringent new laws aimed at reducing "nonessential" packaging by more than 50,000 tons a year, mostly by allowing the country's very green-minded shoppers to take excess wrapping materials back to retail outlets, which must accept them. EC countries collectively recycled 18 percent of their packaging waste in 1991, but hope to raise that figure to 60 percent by early in the next decade.

Germany's well-established engineering and technical excellence have combined with a need to address environmental challenges in a splendid enomic fashion when it comes to air pollution control equipment. The country has become the world's leader in many facets of this technology. In fact, an estimated three-quarters of the new air pollution control equipment installed in American factories today is made in Germany.

Looking farther afield, every EC country and all the other nations of Western and Northern Europe are experiencing a wave of enomic change. In 1991, according to the Organization for Economic Cooperation and Development (OECD), total European environmental business generated $54 billion in revenues. This sum is expected to rise to almost $80 billion by the year 2000.

To this obvious manifestation of enomics may be added the endless positive and negative enomic consequences related to large-scale conversions to natural gas, possible greenhouse taxes, higher costs for fish because of pollution of traditional fishing grounds, and new enomically sound high-speed rail systems. Truly, whatever the political fortunes of West Europe's "green" parties may be in years to come, the environmentalization of West Europe's economics will only strengthen.

What then are the most important enomic lessons American business and government leaders can learn from studying environment-linked economic transformations occurring elsewhere in the world?

- From Japan, the merit of government-industry cooperation rather than confrontation when it comes to greening an economy, and the dangers that can accrue when a nation allows itself to become overly dependent on enomically questionable technologies like those associated with nuclear power.

- From the old Soviet Union, the here-and-now ecological and economic horrors that appear when too many "experts" for too long ignore enomic realities in pursuit of ideological purity.

- From Mexico, the importance of middle-class psychology (a form of greening consumer preferences) in bringing about enomic changes that exclusively ecological or competitive factors cannot bring about directly.

- From Germany, the impossibility of "exporting" waste problems in today's world and the inevitable comeuppance from such past practices.

- From Third World nations, the futility of treating "the environment" as just another way to pick the pockets of more developed nations, when new enomic realities offer potentially far richer prospects.

There are, of course, many other lessons to be learned by pursuing this line of inquiry in other nations, from Great Britain to China, from the Indian subcontinent to the tip of Latin America. All enomic transformations are very different in detail. All, however, are very similar in their underlying inevitability.

PAIN AND DISTRACTIONS

Previous chapters of this book have considered enomics, the new environmental economics, from a variety of perspectives. It is defined as an economics that is environmentally sustainable, an environmentalism that contributes significantly to economic growth.

It is identified as a natural and inevitable economic expression of changed biological imperatives. It is described as a more evolved form of economic activity based on efficient rather than prolific production. It is dubbed "below-the-navel economics" to suggest how it takes into account the nasty, unavoidable, back-end cleanup costs so characteristic of pollution-based manufacturing and transportation—costs that classical economic models long ignored and that current economists tend to underestimate, fail to recognize in all their many guises, or still address using theoretical terms.

In keeping with the notion that all institutions (including economic ones) are largely shaped by the cultural and historical matrices in which they develop, most of the enomic studies in these pages focus on a single geographic model: the environmental restructuring of the American economy. This restructuring is treated as an already very well established and pervasive phenomenon, rather than a futuristic set of aspirations.

To validate this view, existing enomic changes and trends apparent in dozens of key industries and sectors of the economy today are examined. So, too, are enomic-linked changes in the way goods are made, the way they are sold, and the dynamics of the environmental cleanup sector—a sector whose fortunes are but a single thread in the enomic mosaic.

The influence of enomic forces on economic development in different parts of the United States are profiled. Largely in order to clarify the ongoing American enomic experience, a few enomic studies taking place in other parts of the world are likewise discussed in an abbreviated fashion in our previous chapter.

This *Great American Enomic Revolution* is treated throughout this book as an overwhelmingly positive event as well as an inevitable one, a purely economic reality that in essence is merely a better way to do something that with every passing year, with every jump in population, with every extension and elaboration of industrial and transporation systems, has become more and more important: the safe and efficient handling of society's discards.

Such an approach has been followed because it is by and large true. In matters this complex, however, "truth" comes with many caveats. These, too, merit serious attention.

There is a downside to the enomic force, after all, at least in the near term. Pain and anger come in wake of enomic change. Failure to appreciate and address this set of realities, simply to preserve an argument's ideological "purity," would serve only to deny innocent bystanders in the way of inevitable change an appropriate recognition—and perhaps, serve as well to encourage opposition to enomic progress longer than otherwise necessary.

In this chapter, therefore, we look at the now and future dislocations and disruptions that are part and parcel of America's enomic revolution. In addition, we look at the intellectual distractions slowing progress toward achieving our national enomic destiny.

Most people dislike and distrust economists. The reasons are not hard to fathom. This professional caste has an extraordinary penchant for guessing wrong, for predicting soft landings of economic expansions that collapse with a thud, and for heralding the end of recessions that continue to drag on for years after their official demise.

Economists irritate people because of their *modus operandi* as well, which often bear uncanny resemblances to practices employed by astrologers of old. Both economists and astrologers lay claim to a higher wisdom because of the sophisticated mathematical models they use in their work—the one used to track economic performance, the other planetary transits and other astral motions.

Like astrologers, today's economists tend to attach themselves to powerful but insecure individuals in business and government who use these well-paid hirelings both as crutches and whipping boys. Like astrologers too, economists invariably couch their predictions in vague terms that allow various future face-saving interpretations.

What grates the public most about the profession of economist, however, is tied less to inaccuracies or techniques than to the practitioners' perceived cruelty and insensitivity. A "restructuring" spoken of so cavalierly by an economist can translate into enormous personal distress for millions of people. A "recovery" so obvious on an economist's charts and tables may actually be just a continuation of penny-pinching and unrelieved hard times for lesser mortals.

All these things, which are true of economists in general, are equally true of *some* of those who today espouse an enomic form of economics. The pain of readjusting to new enomic realities in this country has become acute for some people, chronic for many, and present in one form or another at some time or another for almost everyone.

The 33,000 logging jobs loudly proclaimed to be in danger during the 1992 presidential campaign because of a need to protect spotted owls was certainly an exaggeration. The 300,000 autoworker jobs said to be in peril during that same campaign if mandatory fuel efficiency standards were raised was a near-total fabrication. Yet many Americans, in the near term, *are* losing jobs because of costs to comply with environmental regulations and other manifestations of environmental restructuring.

This trend is especially pronounced in the mining, petrochemical, and agricultural sectors. It also is closely associated in the public mind with manufacturing job losses. (Just 17 percent of the American work force was employed in manufacturing in 1992, compared to 22 percent in 1980.) It is felt most keenly in parts of the country like Appalachia, sections of the Southwest and California, and the Gulf Coast hydrocarbon belt.

It would be crazy if many people in these industries and regions did not hold a grudge against proponents of enomics— people who are all too easily mistaken for just another brand of old-style environmentalist. To tell victims of a necessary and inevitable transformation that it will all work for the best in the long run is to ignore the famous dictim of the English economist John Maynard Keynes, who observed: "In the long run . . . we are all dead."

The rationalization of wastehandling in American society, which is such a vital element in this country's overall enomic changeover, is another source of friction between enomic thinkers and a host of working-class Americans. "Privatization," most notably in the field of trash collection, is crucial in the efficient collection, transportation, burial, incineration, or recycling of all sorts of used materials. Privatization is thus a delight for enomic boosters.

But among municipal workers, privatization goes by another name: "union-busting." Part of the enomic revolution, it must be acknowledged, involves replacing well-paid, generously benefited municipal employees with low-paid private workers enjoying far fewer job-related benefits. Why would any longtime municipal trash collector seeing a middle-class life-style slip away view this loss favorably?

For many Americans, the psychic hurts among many near-term losers in the enomic sweepstakes are equally hard to bear. It simply is not the same for a former logger to earn his keep collecting pinecones to be used as home decorations during the holiday season or to collect wild mushrooms for sale in organic food stores. Former steelworkers lose something more than income when they are vocationally recycled as hairdressers or hamburger flippers. Coal miners in years past who today must squeak by selling fruits and vegetables to tourists from roadside stands in Kentucky experience a resentment that transcends economic loss.

The politically correct may belittle such attitudes and feelings. Macho men, however, and macha women for that matter, have as much right to their personal myths as more sensitive members of society. And there is no getting around the fact that some of the worst polluting trades of years past were also jobs that gave a certain type of person a sense of deep personal worth.

Elsewhere in this book, environmental regulation is presented not as a punishment for polluters but as a kind of industry policy that gets American business to do something it should be doing anyway—become more efficient (less wasteful of energy and raw materials) and take steps that lessen future environment-related expenditures (adopt intelligent life-cycle planning). In Chapter 6 we also highlight the wonderful new small-business opportunities being generated by a greening economy.

The actual operation of the regulatory process, however, often has innumerable negative consequences for a great many Americans. In some cases, people are merely inconvenienced because they cannot hold outdoor barbeques during smoggy summer days. In extreme cases, however, other people may not even be able to drive to work because of bureaucrat-mandated smog alerts.

Many small-business people are likewise inconvenienced

or more seriously ground down. Like the American system of taxation, which is among the most regressive in the world because it caps the amount the rich must pay in social security exactions while applying the social security tax bite to the entire income of the poor, the American environmental regulatory system is very regressively weighted against smaller companies.

Though big-name polluters complain the loudest about these government mandates, the *Wall Street Journal* recently noted: "Large corporations typically have in-house experts to guide the company through the maze. But most small businesses lack the staff and resources required to track the avalanche of paper from environmental agencies."

In cataloging the real, down-to-earth reasons that real Americans might find today's enomic changes so painful and even infuriating, as opposed to the purely ideological violates-the-free-market-ethic palaver used to justify opposition to enomics during the Reagan-Bush years, questions of personal freedom and disguised taxation also emerge. Like all great and necessary transformations, enomics the worthy principle has often been bastardized for the worst of bureaucratic reasons into enomics the government ripoff.

Under the noble banner of "saving the planet," a great number of undeclared tax increases, especially at the level of local government, are blossoming. Some two hundred American communities now have pay-as-you-throw trash collection programs that charge people on a per-barrel basis. Have any of these communities lowered their property taxes to reflect the extra money taken into municipal coffers by these fees? Of course not.

A great many large cities, such as New York, are introducing pay-by-the-gallon water metering. According to a recent study, water rates generally around the country will rise at twice the rate of inflation during the present decade, and much of this increase will take the form of pay-by-the-gallon. Are any of the cities where this is occurring reducing property taxes to reflect the extra money collected in the form of water fees? Of course not.

Paying by the bag for trash does reduce waste and encourage recycling. Paying by the gallon does encourage water conservation. And doubtless, if trash police begin appearing in cities around the nation, as they already have in urban areas on the West Coast, littering will be cut as well. Can anyone doubt, however, that these ecologically worthy programs are also a disguised form of local taxation similar to parking tickets? Or that these taxes-cum-fees are certain to grow?

At the federal level, there is a sinister trend afoot aimed at turning certain types of law enforcement into cash cows for the Treasury and individual agencies in Washington. With the federal deficit four times as large by 1992 as it was when President Reagan took office in 1981, with just the interest payments on the national debt reaching $199 billion annually by 1992, and with traditional revenue-raising methods now in such disfavor, crypto-taxation in the form of fines by the federal government is becoming an art form.

The most blatant efforts here, of course, involve drugs. Finding a few *Cannibus sativa* weeds on a farmer's land has become grounds to seize the property, while a few residual strands of the dreaded drug in the ashtray of a boat have led to similar seizures—followed by government auctions, the proceeds of which accrue to (you guessed it) the agency doing the seizing. Another Federal agency, the Immigration and Naturalization Service, "earned" $63 million in 1993 fining employers of illegal aliens.

Some "polluters" suspect that the stiff fines they are being forced to pay these days also reflect the fiscal needs of government as much as government efforts to protect and preserve natural ecologies. If this is the case, why would anyone suppose that the legions of Americans who see "environmentalism" as a conspiracy designed to cramp their liberties and pick their pockets will substantially decline in years to come?

These few examples of enomic angst are, of course, not designed to diminish in readers' minds the intrinsic worth of a rite of passage so necessary to bring about both environmental and economic health. Indeed, from a certain perspective, these difficulties only serve to highlight the extraordinary dimensions of the process at work. "No pain, no glory," runs a sports maxim with obviously analogous enomic implications.

A great many people, however, want neither pain nor glory. They seek peace, stability, and physical well-being. Enomics may be viewed by some of these people as a threat to all three.

The first stages of the Industrial Revolution favored the world with vast disparities of wealth, horrendous urban poverty, the spread of pollution, and ultimately the emergence of both communism and fascism. Why assume this most recent stage of the world Industrial Revolution, enomics, will be fully realized on the social and political cheap?

One day soon, ecofascists in Eastern Europe may be destroying "alien" institutions such as democracy, which they identify (using a ferociously irrational logic) with past and continued destruction of their motherlands. Today in Central Europe skinheads already attack longhair environmentalists they identify with higher unemployment caused by the closing down of high-polluting facilities. Today in the United States attacks against environmentalists are likewise on the increase for exactly the same reasons.

There is no way, absolutely no way, to totally avoid the real and imagined pain of enomic transformation. It can be acknowledged, confronted, and much ameliorated, however, through the clear articulation of a vision that portrays a brighter economic future at the end of the passage.

Such a vision, its limitations as well as its power, will be discussed in the next chapter. Here we look briefly at some of the outmoded creeds, pseudovisions, and simple distractions now operating in this country, which impede the enomic progress they purport to advance.

With a certain kind of friend, a person does not need enemies. The activities of people adhering to the cult of "social responsibility," a nebulous movement whose most vocal members manufacture soft goods and whose most visible institutions are a few score nonprofit organizations, foundations, and mutual fund houses, perfectly illustrate how the greening of America's economy has been, and continues to be, impeded by people proclaiming this greening to be one of their primary goals.

"One" is the key word here, because social responsibility adherents have several other goals that are accorded equal time and effort with environmental preservation and restoration. They have, in other words, an agenda. They have "screening criteria" reflecting this agenda. They have deep and abiding moral feelings that keep them from supporting entities that cannot pass through *all* their screens, most especially entities such as those horrible people who actually handle toxic material and pick up the trash rather than just write position papers on the subject.

Such approaches are wondrously counterproductive when it comes to addressing real-world problems related to maintaining physical and chemical balances that preserve life on this planet. Or, for that matter, in helping to maintain conditions needed to support human civilization.

The primary failure of social responsibility thinking, however, is to put "the environment" on a good works agenda in the first place. The environment is not a good work. It is the precondition for all works, good and otherwise. It is no more a moral issue than eating or breathing are moral issues.

Screening mechanisms that impede the flow of capital into necessary environmental technologies or cleanup operations because owners or users of these technologies fail to meet corollary standards involving day care and minority hiring, are therefore hopelessly homocentric—and ecologically inappropriate.

What makes socially responsible efforts on behalf of the environment not merely silly but damaging is the old either/or paradigm such efforts so clearly evoke, the old environment-or-economy choice this book and other enomic tracts are working to supersede. The essence of enomic thinking is that it makes perfect sense for the socially *ir*responsible as well as their more enlightened brethren; that it is fast becoming the doctrine of first-rate managers currently producing wealth, not just a social laundering agent of well-heeled scions of old and new wealth who can finally afford to be nice.

Social responsibility environmentalism is a 1970s sort of thing keeping Americans from focusing on 1990s enomic realities. These realities will win out in any case, of course, but rather more to the economic benefit of our friends in Japan and Germany than ourselves, unless we see them in a truer light devoid of social responsibility blinders.

The same sort of commonsense objections can be applied to the activities of another group of well-meaning professionals now working to save the environment. Under the banner of "ecological economists," these academics and theorists seek to assign dollar values to clear air and pure water, so as to offset the supposed economic advantages that accrue from polluting practices.

Why do they feel this is necessary? And how valid are these feelings? In his 1992 book *Earth in the Balance*, (then) Senator Al Gore quotes World Bank economist Herman Daly thus: "There is no point of contact between macroeconomics and the environment."

If there were, indeed, no point of contact between macroeconomics and the environment, it would, indeed, be difficult for existing economic systems to pursue environmentally sound policies. But since, as noted throughout these pages, trillions of dollars will be spent in this decade around the world on environmental cleanup, since the largest conference of world leaders in human history recently focused on environmental concerns and their economic ramifications, and since the official government-industry policies of world-class economies such as Germany and Japan, together with policies of economic blocs such as the European Community, today embody enomic thinking, the notion that macroeconomics is totally oblivious to the subject seems somewhat strained.

Another spokesman in this field, Robert Costanza, director of the Maryland International Institute for Ecological Economics, wrote in a recent issue of the *Society for Environmental Journalists Journal*: "We must develop better methods to model and value ecological goods and services, and devise politics to translate these values into appropriate incentives. *If we continue to segregate ecology and economics we are courting disaster"* (emphasis added).

Are we truly still segregating ecology and economics? Virtually the entire contents of this book suggest otherwise. Can such segregation be said to exist in the United States today when between $1.2 and $1.5 trillion will be spent in this decade alone on domestic environmental cleanup, when every major component of the U.S. economy is undergoing an environment-linked transformation, and when asset values from stocks to real estate are today so environmentally sensitive?

The current questing beast of ecological economists is a "Green National Product." It seeks to assign value to unpolluted and uncontaminated natural resources, supposedly to balance the current practice of valuing resources only after they are converted into goods and energy (often producing extensive pollution in the process). This approach is quite simply an intellectual playtoy of economist-scholastics. Indeed, this proposed mechanism's most likely real-world consequence would be to attract more grants and conference speaking honoria to its proponents.

The fact that current gross national products and gross domestic products do not reflect the value of clean air and pure water no more requires that these systems be replaced with green national products than the fact that a stethoscope does not measure body temperature but only heartbeat means that stethoscopes have no value as medical tools. Current economic gauges *do* measure environmental damages, not by giving positive worth to uncontaminated assets but by attaching negative worth to contaminated ones. These measurements may not show up in GNPs or GDPs, but they certainly show up on other economic charts and tables.

Such negatives appear on company books in the form of lower real estate values, out-of-pocket fines, lost sales to customers seeking greener products, and less efficient operations that make one firm less competitive than others within the same industry. They also leap out from spreadsheets when one does a life-cycle analysis in which long-term environmental costs are given anywhere near their just due.

If current government and economist policymakers cannot extrapolate from these standard corporate bellweathers, simply because they are not conveniently tucked into gross national product figures, perhaps they should not be entrusted to make policy.

Ecological economics is a kind of New Age epicycle designed to rescue a malfunctioning Ptolemaic economics. It is an attempt to reinvent something that is perceived to be ecologically inappropriate. Enomics, on the other hand, seeks to reinvent nothing. It is merely a set of empirical observations that sensible people ignore at their own environmental and economic peril.

Like social responsibility cultism, ecological economics scholasticism is a distraction from enomic empiricism. Also like social responsibility cultism, it contributes to the massive distrust for authority felt by people whose pain is linked to enomic change.

Ecological economics is the old elitist environmentalism. It is the old Brahmin environmentalism, the old ecofabianism, espoused this time not by people who are merely preaching but by those who aspire to control the economic levers, thus attaining power to make the pain of others worse than it need be by initiating actions that appear to average Americans to have no commonsense basis or relation to everyday life.

This approach stands in stark contrast to the populist environmentalism of enomics. Even government and economist policymakers who cannot recognize enomics' economic reality ought to understand its political utility in reaching out to the still unconverted.

Some of the distractions that keep people from focusing on new enomic imperatives and opportunities involve factors that have been quite significant in the Enomic Revolution during years past, but whose comparative importance is now waning.

The three factors that come to mind at once in this regard are regulation, litigation, and taxation.

Government environmental regulations have, of course, been mightily important for decades in reshaping the way American business has functioned. Regulations have changed a great many bottom-line numbers and provided all sorts of incentives to practice environmentally sound methods, along with providing disincentives to pursue unsound methods. This will certainly continue to be the case in the 1990s and beyond, as new environmental laws and the bureaucratic regulations they necessitate come into being, and as the follow-up provisions of old laws find bureaucratic expression.

Enomics takes these facts into account, but mostly as "done deals." They are givens, background sounds in a marketplace where the attention of the audience is being riveted by a very different score performed on center stage.

There are regulations (including environmental regulations) just as there are taxes. Regulations are important to all businesses but, except on rare occasions, are not absolutely critical to ongoing business success.

Today the danger comes from mistaking regulation for the only (or even the most important) cause of enomic change. Government policymakers who think that promoting enomic objectives primarily means tougher and meaner regulatory enforcement are not only failing to see the enomic marketplace factors that have come into play in recent years but may well miss splendid chances to work cooperatively rather than confrontationally with business in reaching mutually desirable environmental and economic goals.

Environmental litigation also shows all the signs of continuing at present levels. Again, though, as a mechanism to achieve enomic ends, its importance is much less than it used to be.

At a certain point in enomic history, lawyers played a key role in transforming strong but nebulous environmental desires felt by the American people and expressed through their elected representatives into a concrete system with rules that guided corporate and municipal behavior. Litigation was the wake-up call many polluters needed to jolt them from the lethargy of inefficient and wasteful polluting. Court-mandated awards were the painful round of therapy many businesspeople required to understand the need to give their enterprises a greener tinge.

Today, however, the sheer volume of environmental lawyering outweighs most positive enomic consequences of litigation. Just as a glass or two of wine during dinner is an excellent aid to digestion while a fifth of Southern Comfort before noon is a symptom of disease, what was good litigation enomics in moderation is proving to be poisonous in excess.

The crushing weight of environment-linked legal costs is putting many worthwhile smaller enterprises out of business. Some 90 percent of monies paid by insurers on Superfund claims in the last dozen years have gone to attorneys and other legal overhead, according to the RAND Corporation, rather than to actual cleanup. You could die awaiting payments for certain asbestos-caused illness while lawyers run up their hourly billing. Many people have.

There are a number of obvious remedies to litigation problems today as they affect environmental cleanup and pollution prevention. These include judicial reforms limiting attorneys' fees and taking conflicts over who pays how much for which cleanup out of the court system altogether, and replacing them with direct taxes on business to fund government-run remediation projects. If the RAND numbers are anywhere near accurate, this latter approach would achieve roughly ten times the cleanup for the same amount of spending.

What keeps this obvious from becoming actual, however, is not a lack of intelligence and imagination among would-be reformers, nor even the organized opposition of legal associations. It is simply that like the consensus urge of the Japanese, which is both a national strength and a weakness, the litigation urge of Americans is part of our own national psyche.

Some societies are soldier-ridden because their people like order and automatically support institutional violence. Some are priest-ridden because their people are fascinated by ritual.

Ours is lawyer-ridden because Americans are hooked on notions of "fairness" and "morality."

When it comes to the environment, we veer away from the kind of pragmatism pursued by the supposedly fanatical Japanese. We remain obsessed, instead, with fairly allocating blame and punishing the morally deficient.

Litigation is only the means used to act out this national obsession. This being so, environmental law, viewed elsewhere in these pages as an entrepreneurial opportunity for attorneys, will never again provide anything but an occasional boost in bringing about overall enomic progress on these shores. Far more frequently in years to come, it will be a distraction or a series of minifarces comprising a kind of national enomic theater of the absurd.

Once upon a time, taxes played an important role in shaping the direction of this country's overall economic development. Until the so-called reform law passed by Congress in 1986, there were preferences built into the tax code designed to direct money into socially and economically favored sectors of the economy. In order to qualify for a smaller tax bite, wealthy Americans with incomes taxed at the top 50 percent marginal rate were obliged to invest in preferenced investments, such as low-income housing, oil and gas drilling, research and development, and equipment used by manufacturers to upgrade their facilities.

The 1986 Tax Reform Act changed all that. It drastically reduced top marginal tax rates from 50 to 28 percent, while doing away with tax shelter vehicles high-income Americans had long employed to take advantage of preferenced investments that reduced their annual payments to Uncle Sam. This much-ballyhooed trade-off, however, which proponents claimed socked it to the rich by abolishing tax shelters, was really more like taking away someone's right to wear gloves after giving that person a house in Hawaii.

Why would anyone need a tax shelter if his taxes were lowered enough to make sheltering unnecessary? And why would anyone invest in uneconomical low-income housing, or risky oil and gas drilling, if there was no longer a tax advantage to doing so?

This reform, in other words, was a classic shell game the Reagan administration played and Congress went along with during the 1980s, in order to foster trickle-down economics. Among the more obvious results of this policy was a huge increase in homelessness, because low-income housing was no longer subsidized.

American enomics too was indirectly affected by this bizarre "reform." With oil and gas drilling tax subsidies reduced or abolished, domestic drilling fell precipitously. Whether one applauded or condemned this fact, it had very definite enomic consequences. The loss of R&D subsidies slowed American participation in certain key green technologies. Less money also was available for new plants and equipment after 1986, which certainly had enomic spin-offs.

Today hardly an element of the American tax system deliberately or aggressively favors enomic behavior. American corporations that purchase pollution control equipment, for example, are not favored with accelerated depreciation nor do they receive special tax credits. Indeed, they are currently able to write off costs of pollution control equipment just one-third as quickly as corporations in Taiwan and only about half as quickly as companies in Korea.

Green taxes, designed to make environmentally unsound practices less economically viable by introducing the polluter-pays principle into the marketplace, have become popular throughout the industrialized world—except in this country, which still largely depends on regulation to achieve the same end.

In our last chapter we noted how tax policies in Japan and legislation in Germany are bringing about enomic results. France also has tax laws penalizing water polluters, as well as a unique law taxing companies according to the quantity of effluent they release into the air.

Sweden taxes polluters in a way that eliminates any competitive advantage they might derive from such practices. The multination European Community, meanwhile, is introducing a score of taxes that will affect the collective enomic behavior of its member states.

Several of these taxing measures might be introduced in the United States with short-term benefits to the Treasury and longer-term benefits to American corporations by encouraging them to reduce wasteful emissions. What makes such potentially good policy "a distraction" is the likelihood that nothing of the sort will actually happen here soon.

Tax credits of the kind that brought forth heavy investment in new technologies in years past are now largely precluded by a federal deficit whose interest payments alone will shortly be the largest single item in the federal budget. The American tax code generally has been so blatantly footballed for so long in pursuit of so many ephemeral and venal objectives that another major footballing in the early 1990s to produce significant enomic ends (other than conservation via higher gasoline or BTU taxes) is neither feasible nor desirable.

Perhaps the most interesting distraction when it comes to advancing enomic aims involves a category of government-sponsored programs called "emissions credit trading." The interest here lies in the absolute craziness of this policy in relation to the goal it is supposed to achieve.

Anyone of normal intelligence above the age of five understands that the worst way to reduce pollution is to allow the worst polluters to buy their way out of complying with environmental regulations. Yet such is exactly what emissions credit trading encourages.

The rationale for this policy is that such trading will supposedly harness the forces of the free market in pursuit of environmental objectives. When applied to airborne emissions, for example, companies able to reduce their own pollution below mandated levels generate "credits," which the government permits them to sell on "smog exchanges" to companies unwilling or unable to meet these same standards.

The theory here is that the most efficient corporations—the ones that can meet environmental standards in the most cost-effective manner—will have a market incentive to exceed pollution standards by ever-increasing amounts in order to generate ever larger credits for themselves. The net pollution reduction for society as a whole will therefore be greater than what might be realized from uniformly applied standards. The cost to American business as a whole also will be less.

What's wrong with this much acclaimed free market approach to pollution reduction? In the real world, practically everything.

At a time when so many Americans believe that those with enough money and connections can buy their way out of anything, emissions trading seems to prove this is exactly the case when it comes to polluting. If it is inconvenient for you, Mr. Polluter, to comply with the law, hire someone else to do it for you. Surely this is not a message today's American government wishes to convey.

The "average air quality" that emissions trading is designed to improve when it comes to pollutants like sulfur dioxide is itself just a bureaucratic fiction. There is no such thing as "average air quality." No one breathes averages. One breathes the air where one does his or her breathing.

If a utility in Tennessee sells an emissions credit to a utility in Minnesota, people living near the latter are going to continue breathing bad air. This may be fine for some bureaucrat in Washington who can point to a chart and speak of average improvements in air quality. But how about the asthmatic in Minneapolis living next to the utility that bought its way out of compliance?

To see the absurdity of this theory in practice, one need only image that the same averaging principle used in emissions credit trading were applied to fire safety. Imagine living in a city where half the buildings did not have fire escapes, because their owners had purchased "fire safety credits" from other building owners who not only met fire escape standards but also installed sprinkler systems. Would such a system improve the overall fire safety in this city?

In purely environmental terms, the prime drawback of emissions credit trading is that the companies selling them are *not*, in fact, goaded into more prolific improvements of their own emissions record by the lure of creating saleable credits. There are countless actions that could generate tradable credits which have nothing to do with a conscious effort to reduce pollution below legally mandated standards.

A company could, for example, install a new piece of equipment purely to boost production, and if that equipment just happens to be more efficient in its operations and therefore less polluting, a credit is produced. A company could even generate a credit by closing down one of its plants—a splendid way for incompetent management to recoup some of its losses through the creation of ersatz assets.

Virtually all pollution credits, in fact, will be sold by companies getting an artificial return for things they would have done anyway, a return paid for by companies that find it inconvenient to comply with pollution control laws and regulations. The net effect of this process on this country's environment will of course be negative.

The net enomic effect will be even more negative. Instead of finally coming to grips with new market realities that make environmentally sound and economically sound behavior synonymous, companies are encouraged by this government-sponsored policy to delay intelligent and progressive investments in real efficiency.

Alas, the very inanity of emissions trading seems only to increase its appeal. The EPA in Washington supports this approach and has backed a system permitting utilities to engage in trading certain pollutants covered by the 1990 Clean Act Act. The South Coast Air Quality District in Los Angeles has a comparable program in the works. The packaging used by the system's promoters has made it irresistible to such government entities.

In the 1960s, if you wanted to get a government program favoring your own interests put on the books, you made it out to be part of the War on Poverty. In the 1970s, you called it vital for Energy Independence. In the early 1980s, almost any program could be funded if it were part of the Great Defense Buildup.

In the 1990s, the magic phrases guaranteed to fuzz the

thinking of legislators and put a sparkle in the eyes of bureaucrats are "free market solution" and "public-private partnership." That pollution credit trading is neither, that it is a head game of academics and a new product line for former junk bond peddlers, is no more an impediment to its widespread acceptance than the inherent silliness of Star Wars hindered research into space-based beam weapons a decade ago.

There *are* some government-sponsored, market-based incentives that would promote real-world enomic ends. A number of changes in the tax code, better regulatory policies, and more finely honed litigation targets also might hasten enomic progress.

Social responsibility thinking does have some merit in boosting green buying preferences among consumers. Even creating green national product measuring systems to complement rather than replace traditional gross national product and gross domestic product systems might have utility in raising enomic consciousness among officials who employ this kind of gauge in their work.

What makes all of these approaches distractions, however, is that they all ignore or detract from the perception that enomic reality already exists, that its growing importance is inevitable, that it is an inherently desirable phenomenon, and that the present pain of enomic transformation presages economic well-being as well as ecological preservation.

Enomics is no longer something that needs to be invented, nor can its implications be avoided. Every attempt to "save the planet" by sacrificing the economy is a delusion. Every policy or technique that advances or helps perpetuate this delusion is counterproductive.

In our final chapter, we look at some things that government *can* do and is beginning to do to foster and make less painful enomic change and how people in business can realize their own full enomic potential most quickly. We also put enomics into the context of a far larger environmental upheaval that affects, and is affected by, shifting patterns of institutional behavior around the planet.

ELEVEN

MODEST PROPOSALS, LIMITED VISIONS

Most revolutions are really evolutions. They take place over decades, or even centuries, with history tending to focus only on their most violent and traumatic episodes, the ones most neatly compressible into easily chronicled spans of time.

The French Revolution of the late eighteenth century actually settled very few of the class conflicts it unleashed, and was alive and well in a variety of ways through the 1930s and beyond. The Russian Revolution did not end with the triumph of the Bolsheviks. Indeed, its most active phase may still be in the offing. The Chinese Revolution has already been going for almost a century, and its main political consequences are still not totally clear.

The least violent and hence least "revolutionary" political upheaval of modern times, the American Revolution, today seems to be influencing the most revolutionary efforts of countries around the world. This is true not only in terms of the legislative, democratic examples it is setting for so many nations. Its greatest long-term models for emulation may well turn out to be in the field of federalism, the division of power between a central government and its constituent parts, the problem currently causing so much conflict and even violence from Canada to the old Soviet Union, from the Balkans to the Indian subcontinent.

What is true for political revolutions, of course, is also true for economic ones. The Industrial Revolution in its many guises has been going on for more than 250 years in parts of Europe, and today it continues to ripple through societies on every populated continent. The latest major manifestation of this transformation, the Enomic Revolution, likewise has roots going back many years and a future stretching farther than we can know.

In order to get some sort of comfortable, usable, historical sense of the highly complex and often confusing enomic events now so strongly affecting the U.S. economy, however, it is probably best to divide the messiness of real-world enomic change into a few neat time capsules. This is also a good way to see what government policies make the most sense at this juncture of the Enomic Revolution and which attitudes and practices are most appropriate for people in business who are today's true American enomic revolutionaries.

The "big years" in the modern history of world political revolution were 1776, 1789, 1848, 1917, 1948 to 1950, and 1989 to 1990. In the Enomic Revolution, the most important single year to date was 1970, while its most critical multiyear period was 1990 to 1992.

As we have noted, the explosive increase in ecological consciousness that occurred after the first Earth Day in 1970 triggered pro-environmental legislation in every major Western industrial nation and, for largely domestic reasons, in Japan as well. Economics and ecology began to fuse in these nations during the 1970s, though this fusion was still largely obscured by ideologies. In the 1970s, also, there was no nascent fusion between economics and ecology in the Soviet Union, which was one of the primary causes for the disintegration of that nation's economic system a little while later.

An enomic counterrevolution, of sorts, took place in

many countries during the early 1980s. It is most closely associated with the ill-conceived and badly misnamed "free market" anti-environmentalism of the Reagan administration in the United States, though its worst long-term economic consequences in the West may actually turn out to be in Great Britain.

The Dada Enomics of Reaganism was at least partially ameliorated by a federal system of government that permitted large chunks of the United States to experience continuing greening of their local economies even as the national government in Washington was doing everything it could to discourage such greening. In Great Britain, however, a similar Dada enomics occurring under the banner of Thatcherism was able to impose its classical view that pollution and prosperity were synonymous unchecked, and did so with such abandon, that Britain's ecosystems were ravished and its real estate damaged in ways that will depress property values for decades to come.

The enomic counterrevolution in most industrialized nations (outside the Soviet Bloc) began to lose sway by the late 1980s. This occurred largely because government elites in Germany and Japan and business elites in the United States, finally began to appreciate the growing correlations between what produced contemporary wealth (efficiency) and what destroyed wealth (pollution).

Ideological anti-environmentalism also began to fade with the disappearance of Ronald Reagan and Margaret Thatcher from the political scene. A host of simmering ecological problems, meanwhile, resurfaced at this time, and these reignited a popular impulse to "save the planet."

The years 1990 through 1992 saw the final rout of a polite intellectual anti-enomics. In consequence, today it is simply impossible for anyone in a position of power anywhere in the world to speak of highly polluting manufacturing or agriculture as anything other than a near-term necessity, a way of generating the front-end capital needed to put a manufacturing or agriculture system on a more environmentally sustainable path.

The breakup of the Soviet Union, and subsequent revelations about the horrendous environmental-cum-economic damages within its old boundaries and those of its former satellites, contributed much to this changed perception. So did the extraordinary economic success during the 1980s of Japan and Germany. Both produced more goods per unit of energy and raw materials than their international competitors and, by virtue of these less-wasteful, hence less-polluting practices, became comparatively more prosperous.

Chernobyl and the Valdez oil spill also galvanized thinking when it came to the exorbitant costs of pollution. The United Nations' Rio conference on the environment focused this thinking more narrowly on how to merge economic development with environmental protection.

In the United States, between 1990 and 1992 the best minds in the American business community and the best minds in organized environmentalism finally started coming together regarding the mutual benefits to be realized from a new environmental economics. For businesspeople, the primary impetus here was market forces related to world competitive pressures, changing customer tastes, and the big dollars to be made in cleanup. For environmentalists, the key incentive was a very strong desire to stop being political punching bags.

After the defeat of California's "Big Green" referendum in 1990 and similar political defeats all around the country that same year, it finally dawned on America's environmental leadership that one could not sell the concept of saving the earth at the expense of jobs and profits, at a time when worries about jobs and profits among so many Americans made them more concerned with saving themselves than their planetary home.

This perception did not cause a true enomic vision to sweep immediately through the ranks of organized environmentalism. In fact, most American environmentalists still cling to the old "either/or" model in their heart of hearts when it comes to environmental protection and economic growth.

Though they still may not walk-the-walk in this regard, however, since the Big Green fiasco, environmentalists have at least learned to talk-the-talk. By the time the 1992 presidential campaign rolled around, environmental groups finally overcame their official distaste for making (rather than inheriting) money to the extent of offering fulsome support for ultra-clean cleanup technologies such as solar and recycling. Even so, firms that handled trash and toxic wastes, and longtime corporate polluters in the chemical field actively working to green their own operations, were still considered the bad guys, in spite of the transcendental enomic importance of such activities.

The Clinton-Gore administration thus came to power in early 1993 with an extraordinary enomic opportunity. Rabid anti-enomics was dead. The old environment-or-economy way of thinking was still alive and well among many of its traditional environmentalist and business adherents, but it was no longer a point of view to be bandied about in polite political company. In this ideological vacuum, it was possible to abet an enomic transformation that prior administrations had either ignored or retarded.

The political landscape was finally open to a clear, concise, and forceful articulation of a true American enomics. The time was ripe for a call to link the rejuvenation of the U.S. economy to the regeneration of natural planetary systems. It was possible to create a synthesis of national economic pride, technological leadership, entrepreneurial excellence, and a post–Cold War vision with truly global implications.

This articulation, more than any program of green taxation or expanded environmental regulation, could with the coming of a new administration, become an officially recognized enomic policy in the United States. Surely, if the false vision of communism could sustain so many hopes for so long in so many parts of the world, and permit a self-proclaimed "vanguard" to indulge in bungled goverance with at least the passive acquiesence of a majority of Soviet citizens, a properly delineated enomic vision would now permit an inevitable ecological and economic transformation to occur on American shores in a far less disruptive manner and in a far more compressed time frame.

What, then, are the enomic policies of choice and (given

current fiscal restraints) of necessity for the Clinton-Gore administration? What are the new enomic policies this administration did begin pursuing, albeit rather tepidly, during its first months in office? They can be summed up in four words: cooperation, recognition, encouragement, and jawboning.

The regulatory process began to be treated as an opportunity for business and government to work together to bring about mutually desirable goals related to productive efficiency, reducing future environmental exposure, and ecologically appropriate behavior. In essence, this means that after a government environmental objective is established, polluters are permitted increasing flexibility in meeting it.

After more than twenty years on the environmental regulation wheel, all parties in this process have learned that while confrontation over regulations does produce enomic results it is a lousy mechanism for doing so. Now that attitudes are finally coming around, now that business and government and the general public are finally realizing that only lawyers and lobbyists benefit when parties are continually pitted against one another to achieve "fairness" and "justice," the stage is set for a much greater degree of enomic cooperation.

Increasingly, administration officials from President Clinton on down are pursuing the "big truth" technique in order to rid Americans of residual misconceptions concerning that old "choice between environment and economy" bugaboo. The presidency has long been used as a bully pulpit to front for narrow interests and shrill theorists in this realm. This pulpit is now at least *starting* to be used to proclaim an enomic message worthy of the podium.

Because the Enomic Revolution is so well and truly advanced today, such education, rather than old-style activism, can be successful. Enomic pitches at major schools, enomic meetings with green business groups, enomic statements from the Departments of Commerce and Interior, as well as the Environmental Protection Agency, are all helping accentuate the enomic proclivities of executives and getting the message out to both Wall Street and Main Street.

Enomics in the United States has long been a bottoms-up, not a tops-down, phenomenon. It was understood by a great many small businesspeople long before environmental leaders, economists, or politicians tumbled to it. Enomic bully pulpiting from above merely closes the loop and helps assure those below that their leaders have at least gotten *this* message.

Equating a greening of the economy too closely with the fortunes of the environmental services/pollution control industry seems to be receding as a misconception within the new administration and as the prime focus of its enomic jawboning. This industry certainly will be a growth sector for the U.S. economy for years to come, and in certain respects, its ability to produce jobs and profits can be likened to that of the defense industry in years past.

Enomics, however, is not just about one industry, no matter how big, no matter how important. An analogy here with the computer industry and the Information Revolution is fairly close.

If not another new computer were sold after today, every business currently using computers would still recognize that processing information more quickly constitutes a competitive edge. If not another old waste site had to be cleaned up after today, progressive businesses would still recognize the value of enomic behavior as a competitive edge.

A lot of people still do not like computers or feel uncomfortable about using them. But almost no one is hostile to the concept of computer literacy or doubts it is a valuable job skill.

Leading lights in a Clinton-Gore administration seem at least modestly attuned to the notion that *environmental* literacy is needed for all jobs. This is, in fact, the essence of employment wisdom in our fast-greening economy. Jawboning from the top on this subject just helps get the idea across a bit quicker.

An inclusive, everyone on board, liberals and conservatives together sharing an enomic dream, is slowly emerging as part of the *vision thing* President Clinton was elected to formulate. Enomics is what the 1990s are supposed to be all about. It is an amalgam of the idealism of the 1960s and the prosperity hopes of the 1980s. Enomic policies that generate enthusiastic cooperation, rather than those that merely encourage sullen obedience, are the quintessential example of such an amalgam.

And then, of course, there is a dawning understanding of what enomic politics could mean for the new administration itself. Not so long ago there was a governor from a small southern state who was elected President of the United States. He came to office with enormously decent inclinations and a head full of very good ideas.

Suddenly he faced a national energy crisis. He opted to confront this crisis with scads of programs and initiatives, but failed to articulate a vision that fired the imagination of the American public. He served one term.

The parallels between President Carter and energy economics and President Clinton and environmental economics are too numerous and obvious to enumerate. In a world filled with spreading disorders, in a country facing fiscal crises, getting out in front of the enomics bandwagon, speeding it along with good words rather than costly and combative bureaucratic activism, then taking credit for inevitable enomic progress that would have occurred anyway, may be the easiest option for an economic home run a Clinton-Gore administration is likely to have for some years to come. There are at least tentative signals from the new administration that this fact is finally appreciated.

Had a sequel been written for Charles Dickens's famous novel *A Christmas Carol,* readers might well have learned that the sober and solid businessman Ebenezer Scrooge, who had been gulled and shamed into an unseemly spasm of charitable good works in the book's original edition, ended his days as an almshouse recluse, while his ne'er-do-well nephew and the Cratchet family consumed his hard-earned wealth in a spectacular burst of consumption.

The chief lesson of such a sequel, of course, one that serious nineteenth-century political reformers in Dickens's own time understood all too well, was that charity is a poor way to improve the long-term prospects of working people. Over any time period lasting longer than a Christmas holiday season, and during a stage of the Industrial Revolution when British goods were fighting for market share in increasingly competitive Continental and New World markets, the only real path toward higher standards of living for Britain's working class in the last century involved higher productivity and technical innovation.

The exact same lesson applies today. Social responsibility thinking among businesspeople when it comes to environmental economics would produce consequences not unlike this neo–*Christmas Carol* sequel. Such thinking is in fact frothy sentimentality of the worst sort because it obstructs a fundamental truth: Enomics is not an alternative to traditional ways of doing business. It is their natural extension.

The place for businesspeople to look for enomic models is therefore among this country's (and the world's) best-run enterprises. Entire chapters of this book do just that. A few generic rules to be gleaned from these models include the following:

The best-run companies today look beyond simple compliance with environmental regulations and toward techniques and procedures that can remove the companies from the compliance wheel altogether at some not-too-distant date. Most frequently, this approach consists of combining full-cycle engineering improvements and life-cycle managerial thinking.

Addressing environmental concerns at the front end of a manufacturing cycle is almost always cheaper and easier than solving back-end environmental problems. Using different materials with less long-term polluting potential, and using less-polluting procedures to turn these materials into finished goods, just plain costs less money overall.

Once enomics is worked into thinking up and down the corporate chain-of-command, it almost always turns out to be a more efficient way to make products. Pollution is sloth. Pollution is laziness. Pollution is underevolved management. Enomics solves all these problems.

In an increasingly internationalized world marketplace, enomics is often the key to expanding a company's export potential. Not only will the tigers of Asia soon emerge as the world's biggest buyers of environmental services and pollution control equipment (green goods), they will become more and more receptive to enomic packaging of all kinds and be ever more prone to purchase products that pollute their own domestic ecosystems less.

Similar patterns are equally evident in the 350 million-person West European Common Market that came into being at the start of 1993. And progressive American marketers can still lock in future enomic markets in largely underdeveloped parts of the world as well.

One day, nations such as Ukraine and the Philippines will begin serious enforcement of their own environmental laws. They will secure enough capital to pay for cleanups, and their citizens will have enough spare cash to favor sellers of goods that are less environmentally destructive. These future enomic markets are being won or lost today by the actions or inactions of the world's multinationals and a host of smaller, feisty entrepreneurs.

One reason American companies have a head start in these now and future offshore enomic markets is because environmental regulations have been applied and enforced in the United States longer than anywhere else. Countless corporate enomic techniques have come into being here that are marketable abroad to enomic newcomers.

Such techniques are rarely included in catalogs of green goods. But they nonetheless constitute a huge potential pool of national assets, which along with the usual litany of envirotech products such as scrubbers and catalytic converters can contribute to corporate bottom lines.

American coal companies, by way of example, have a long and often painful history complying with laws designed to force them to restore polluted mining sites after mines are closed. Coal company executives have expertise growing trees that can survive (and even thrive) in soil heavily contaminated by mine wastes. The American coal industry is also the most advanced in the world when it comes to capturing poisonous methane gas in its mines and turning it into a usable source of energy.

American coal companies will never sell coal to Poland or China, two of the world's largest producers. These same firms, however, might well sell countries like Poland and China their hard-won skills remediating overmined landscapes and turning underground poisons into fuel.

America's corporate inventories contain literally thousands of comparable enomic treasures. The profits to be made selling them in a world market where $3 trillion or $4 trillion will be spent over the course of this decade on environmental cleanup and restoration are incalculable.

As is the case with government policies, corporate enomics is less a matter of specifics than of attitude. And once again, the computer–Information Revolution model applies. Executives who did not see the necessity and utility of employing superior information systems in the 1970s put their enterprises at an enormous competitive disadvantage. Why repeat the same mistake in the 1990s when it comes to enomics?

The proper role for government when it comes to advancing the enomic agenda is a difficult one for politicians, especially legislators and administrators of the Democratic persuasion. While physicians take an oath whose prime directive is "do no harm," and by extension, do little but encourage a patient when that is the best way to achieve a cure, Democratic administrations lean toward activism, even when a largely vocal passive approach is the best way to get the job done. Exercising restraint, moderation and cooperation when it comes to enomics will thus be an ongoing challenge for a new Clinton administration. Judging from early actions of EPA chief Carol Browner, and Interior Secretary Bruce Babbitt, however, perhaps it will not be an impossible challenge to meet.

The proper role for business when it comes to advancing the enomic agenda, on the other hand, involves a far greater degree of activism. All the dominant marketplace trends today are supportive of enomic progress. These include an increased premium on efficient production and manufacture in response to greater competitive pressures, greening consumer demands in this country, burgeoning foreign green markets, the emergence of less polluting technologies, and the like.

By now, alert businesspeople no longer need to be coaxed to think green. Indeed, enomics, under a variety of banners, has become the watchword for America's business self-starters.

In constructing government and business policies that serve the obvious enomic interests of the United States, the chief policy proposals of this book turn out to be surprisingly modest:

Government should focus on the bully pulpit and delineate a vision uniting the needs of business, a passion for nature, a resurgent national pride, individual prosperity, American world leadership, and planetary salvation.

Businesses must focus on doing what American businesses have always done well: making things in the most cost-effective way possible and selling them in the best way possible. Only now businesses must do it better than in years past, in accordance with new enomic marketplace rules of the road.

These two modest-sounding enomic proposals, of course, are not really modest at all in the real world. Here, the inclinations and capacities of well-meaning and not so well-meaning interest groups and their political instruments makes even the most modest and obvious transformations far more difficult than they need be.

T. S. Eliot, in his poem *Hollow Men,* nicely summed up the nature of the difficulty here, noting that a "shadow" often comes between ideas and realities, motions and actions. The shadow in this instance, when it comes to realizing enomic goals, is the inertial deadweight of old ideas and incompetent leadership.

In spite of these givens, enomics, the new environmental economics, will ultimately triumph in this country and around the world. Indeed, to a surprising extent, it already has. If enomic awareness, if the substitution of enomic practices for traditional interactions between the economy and the natural environment, were the main threat to the current order of life on this planet (and the current organization of human civilizations on the planet), "keeping it all together" would merely be a matter of hastening the inevitable.

Alas, there is a great deal more to rectifying the relationship between humans and nature. And here we come back to the idea broached in the very first pages of this book, the idea of economic systems as just one of the human institutions in profound flux today because of new environmental conditions that humanity has created over the last century.

Enomics, it turns out, is the easy part of this grand reordering. The making and transporting and merchandising of goods and services just happens to be moving in an ecologically sound direction (at least in this country) at a fast enough pace so that at least theoretically, with a bit of luck and some vision at the top, we could "have it all," in the sense of widespread material prosperity and natural preservation.

Today other, largely noneconomic institutions present the really intractable difficulties at the human-nature interface. Institutions such as religions, whose best theologians twist themselves into intellectual knots trying to render humanity the stewards of nature without limiting humanity's God-given right to procreate unchecked. Institutions such as nationalism, which wallow in motherland love without the slightest concern for the health of lands and waters beyond its own artificial borders. Institutions such as science, where a devotion to unfettered curiosity often exceeds a sense of environmental integrity.

We have the economic tools and the economic incentives to reinvent our economies along environmental principles no more inherently destructive of natural systems than these systems are of themselves. So many other human institutional tools are lacking, however, that many unpleasantly interesting times await humanity in years to come.

If enomics is thus a vision of limited utility, it is nonetheless one based on realities rather than ideology, and therefore deserving of serious consideration. Like many visions, religious and secular, its basic proposition can also be represented symbolically. In this case, in a single, simple symbol.

Take the statement:

What's good for the environment = What's good for the economy

On the left side of this statement, use the sign for infinity (the constantly regenerative and regenerated natural order) to represent "the environment."

Use the dollar sign with a single bar to represent "the economy" on the right side of the statement.

The equivalency obtained looks like this:

The interesting thing about this equivalency is that it is both symbolically and intellectually equivalent, in that the dollar sign with a single bar *becomes* an infinity symbol when the bar is shifted a few degrees.

The two symbols can then be merged into a single symbol to form a nonsectarian cross. Thus:

This is the totality of the new environmental economics. This is all of enomics. Everything else is commentary.

BIBLIOGRAPHY

Note: Because the Enomic Revolution is a contemporary, on-going phenomenon rather than a historical event, much of the information in these pages is culled from newspapers and other periodicals, along with corporate annual and other reports, rather than from books or from studies prepared by think tanks or government agencies. Facts and statistics were gleaned from more than one thousand newspaper and magazine articles alone. When it seemed appropriate, these sources are cited in the text. A few of the more important of these sources are mentioned generically below. Individual books and lengthier report/article sources are cited by name.

NEWSPAPER AND MAGAZINE SOURCES

Advertising Age
BioCycle
Boston Globe
Christian Science Monitor
Environmental Business Journal

In Business magazine
New York Times
Philadelphia Inquirer
Wall Street Journal
Washington Post

NOTEWORTHY REPORTS AND ARTICLES

Clarke, Stephen F. (Study Coordinator). *The Tax Treatment of Expenditures on Antipollution Equipment and Facilities in Selected Foreign Countries.* Law Library of Congress, 1991.

French, Hillary E. *Green Revolutions: Environmental Reconstruction in Eastern Europe and the Soviet Union.* WorldWatch Paper 99, 1990.

McGill, Douglas C. "Japan's Choice—Scour Technology's Stain with Technology." *New York Times Sunday Magazine*, October 4, 1992, pp. 32–34, 56, 60.

Organization for Economic Cooperation and Development. *The OECD Environmental Industry: Situation, Prospects and Government Policies.* Paris: OECD, 1992.

Thorning, Margo. *International Comparison of the Tax Treatment of Pollution-Control Investment (A Special Report).* American Council for Capital Formation, Center for Policy Research, 1992.

United Nations. *National Strategies and Policies for Air Pollution Abatement.* New York. United Nations, 1987.

Vig, Norman J. and Michael E. Kraft, eds. *Environmental Policy in the 1990s.* Washington, D.C.: Congressional Quarterly, 1990, pp. 257–273.

Wennink, Karel. *Green Taxes in Various Countries.* European Law Division, Law Library of Congress, 1990.

BOOK SOURCES

Bennett, Steven. *Ecopreneuring.* New York: John Wiley & Sons, 1992.

Brin, David. *Earth.* New York: Bantam Books, 1990.

Buckholz, R., and A. Marcus. *Managing Environmental Issues: A Casebook*, Englewood Cliff, NJ: Prentice Hall, 1992.

Cairncross, Frances. *Costing the Earth: The Challenges for Government—The Opportunities for Business.* Boston: Harvard Business School Press, 1992.

Carless, Jennifer. *Renewable Energy. A Concise Guide to Green Alternatives.* New York: Walker and Company, 1993.

Carson, Patrick and Julia Moulden. *Green Is Gold.* Toronto: HarperBusiness, 1991.

Carson, Rachel. *Silent Spring.* Boston: Houghton Mifflin, 1962.

CEIP Fund. *The Complete Guide to Environmental Careers.* Washington, D.C.: Island Press, 1992.

Cohn, Susan. *Green at Work.* Washington, D.C.: Island Press, 1992.

Congressional Budget Office. *Environmental Regulation and Economic Efficiency.* Washington, D.C.: 1985.

Eliot, T. S., *Collected Poems,* London: Faber & Gwyer, Ltd., 1925.

Elkington, John, Julia Hailes, and Joel Makower. *The Green Consumer.* New York: Penguin Books, 1990.

Erocol, Denizhan. *Environmental Management in Developing Countries.* Paris: OECD, 1991.

Gore, Al. *Earth in the Balance: Ecology and the Human Spirit.* New York: Houghton Mifflin, 1992.

Halberstam, David. *The Next Century.* New York: William Morrow and Co., 1991.

Kolluru, Rao V. *Environmental Strategies Handbook.* New York: McGraw-Hill, 1993.

Management Institute for Environment and Business. *Business and the Environment: A Resource Guide.* Washington, D.C.: Island Press, 1991.

Organization for Economic Cooperation and Development. *Environmental Labelling in OECD Countries.* Paris: OECD, 1991.

Ottman, J. *Green Marketing: Challenges and Opportunities for the New Marketing Age.* Chicago: NTC Business Books, 1993.

Schmidheiny, Stephan, with the Business Council for Sustainable Development. *Changing Course.* Cambridge, MA: MIT Press, 1992.

Schumacher, E. F. *Small Is Beautiful: Economics as if People Mattered.* New York: Harper & Row, 1973.

Shabecoff, Philip. *A Fierce Green Fire.* New York: Hill & Wang, 1993.

Silverstein, Michael. *The Environmental Factor.* Chicago: Longman, 1989.

Silverstein, Michael. *The Environmental Industry Yearbook and Investment Guide.* Philadelphia: Environmental Economics, 1992.

Tietenberg, Tom. *Environmental and Natural Resources Economics* (Third Edition). New York: HarperCollins, 1992.

INDEX